DIVE INTO UDL

Immersive Practices to Develop Expert Learners

Kendra Grant
and Luis Perez

International Society for Technology in Education

PORTLAND, OREGON • ARLINGTON, VA

Dive into UDL
Immersive Practices to Develop Expert Learners
Kendra Grant and Luis Perez
© 2018 International Society for Technology in Education

Acquisitions Editor: *Valerie Witte*
Developmental and Copy Editor: *Linda Laflamme*
Proofreader: *Steffi Drewes*
Indexer: *Wendy Allex*
Book Design and Production: *Mayfly Design*
Cover Design: *Eddie Ouellette*

Library of Congress Cataloging-in-Publication Data available

First Edition
ISBN: 978-1-56484-665-5
Ebook version available

Printed in the United States of America

ISTE® is a registered trademark of the International Society for Technology in Education.

About ISTE

The International Society for Technology in Education (ISTE) is the premier nonprofit organization serving educators and education leaders committed to empowering connected learners in a connected world. ISTE serves more than 100,000 education stakeholders throughout the world.

ISTE's innovative offerings include the ISTE Conference & Expo, one of the biggest, most comprehensive edtech events in the world—as well as the widely adopted ISTE Standards for learning, teaching and leading in the digital age and a robust suite of professional learning resources, including webinars, online courses, consulting services for schools and districts, books, and peer-reviewed journals and publications. Visit iste.org to learn more.

Join our community of passionate educators

ISTE members get free year-round professional development opportunities and discounts on ISTE resources and conference registration. Membership also connects you to a network of educators who can instantly help with advice and best practices.

Join or renew your ISTE membership today!

Visit iste.org/membership or call 800.336.5191.

Related ISTE Titles

The New Assistive Tech, by Christopher R. Bugaj

To see all books available from ISTE, please visit iste.org/resources.

About the Authors

Kendra Grant has held many roles in education, including teacher, district special education coordinator and assistive technology (AT) specialist in a large school district. She currently works with Quillsoft as director of professional development and learning, and was formerly co-founder and chief education officer for a professional learning company delivering large-scale technology implementation across North America. Grant holds a master's of educational technology from the University of British Columbia with a focus on professional learning, eLearning (K-20) and the application of UDL to both. She is a past president of ISTE's Inclusive Learning Network.

Luis Pérez is a technical assistance specialist for the National Center on Accessible Educational Materials at CAST. In this role, he promotes the creation, delivery, and use of high-quality accessible educational materials and technologies that support equitable learning opportunities for all students. He holds a doctorate in special education and a master's degree in instructional technology from the University of South Florida. While at USF, he was also project manager for Tech Ease for All, a collection of free assistive technology and web accessibility resources for educators from the Florida Center for Instructional Technology. Luis was selected as an Apple Distinguished Educator (ADE) in 2009, and he currently serves as President-Elect of ISTE's Inclusive Learning Network, which named him its 2016 Outstanding Inclusive Educator.

Acknowledgments

We want to thank several individuals who have been instrumental in making this book possible:

- Our dear friend, colleague, and travel partner Elizabeth Dalton, who worked with us on the online course that provided much of the inspiration for this book.
- Our good friend (and voice-over artist extraordinaire) at CAST, Mindy Johnson, who so graciously shares her insight and deep knowledge of UDL. She truly is a #UDLrockstar!
- Our #InclusiveLN PLN. Their tireless work to promote inclusion in the educational technology community motivates us to push forward in our quest to create more equitable learning opportunities for all students.
- Our editor Linda Laflamme, whose thoughtful feedback and guidance made the process of writing the book such an enjoyable one.
- The team at ISTE, including Valerie Witte, for supporting our vision to bring inclusive learning and UDL to the broader ISTE community.

Finally, our loved ones who put up with our late hours and understood the personal meaning this work has for the two of us.

KENDRA:

To my husband, Rudy, for his unwavering support whenever I take the leap into something new and to my sons, Brad and Jeff, who embrace their amazing jagged profiles.

LUIS:

To my daughter, Katherine, my inspiration and reason for wanting to leave behind a better world. To the memory of my grandmother, Cija, a model of love, strength, and determination throughout her long life.

Contents

PART 1: Your Professional Self

PART 2: UDL and You

PART 3: Inquire, Plan, Act, Reflect

Foreword

first came to know Kendra Grant and Luis Perez through our mutual work in the International Society for Technology in Education (ISTE), which started almost 10 years ago. I remember this distinctly, as it was right after I had finished my Ph.D. and was searching for a way to connect to the world of education beyond Rhode Island, where I had spent most of my professional life. Kendra was an active educational entrepreneur, with her own consulting company. Luis was a newly minted Ph.D., who, like myself, was looking to connect and make a difference in the field. Each of us found our way to the Inclusive Learning Network of ISTE—a group of dedicated and dynamic professionals who were focused on diversity and had a passion for sharing the resources needed to *level the playing field* of education for those with differing needs. This passion led our group boldly into the world of Universal Design for Learning (UDL).

There are many different approaches and frameworks which have emerged over the years to help understand and support learner diversity and how to teach varied learners. Some that you may be familiar with include Carol Tomlinson's *Differentiated Instruction*, Grace Fernald's *Multisensory Instruction (VAKT)*, Howard Gardner's *Theory of Multiple Intelligences,* and Benjamin Bloom's *Taxonomy of Learning,* among others. During a post-doctoral fellowship on UDL with the Center for Applied Special Technology (CAST) and Boston College, I was confronted with the question, "How is UDL different from other educational approaches which help to mitigate learning differences for those with diverse needs?" With many years as a special education teacher and teacher trainer under my belt, I knew this was an important question to answer. After much consideration, I finally came to this conclusion—that *UDL is a framework that can be used to better implement ALL of these approaches.* Soundly based in the body of neuroscientific research on how the brain works, UDL is beautifully practical in its simplicity. This framework is based on three core principles—multiple means of engagement, multiple means of representation, and multiple means of action and expression. The principles are clear and understandable for practitioners, and we can envision how we may better engage our students in the classroom, how we may vary the ways we teach and present our lessons, and how we may design and provide options for students to demonstrate what they have learned.

First developed by CAST in the 1990s, UDL is now recognized both nationally and internationally as a key educational approach that benefits ALL students, since every student varies in the ways that they will learn best. UDL, when clearly understood and effectively implemented, can truly support the learning needs of every student. And this brings us to the tough issue of implementation...always the most challenging task for educators. We know, theoretically, what we *want* to do, but often struggle with how, exactly, we will accomplish this in the reality of our classrooms (or other learning environments). As someone who has spent much of my professional career in the special education and assistive technology worlds, I appreciate the challenge of implementation—and that we, as educators, must recognize this is *where the rubber meets the road*. Without implementation, all theories and frameworks are just words on paper. This is where **DIVE INTO UDL** comes in.

There are other very good books available on UDL. **DIVE INTO UDL** is different. It is a book for the practitioner—at any level of education. Kendra and Luis have pooled their years of expertise to present a text that can help anyone who really wants to understand UDL and put it into practice. The organization of the book first sets the stage with foundations of UDL (*do not skip* the Introduction), and moves right into issues that are most important to us as education professionals. Following this, they guide us on a personalized path to understand UDL, by wading in, doing shallow swims, and taking deep dives. Along the way, you are invited to customize how you use this book, by choosing what to read and how you will read it—THIS IS SO UDL! Finally, the authors lead us, in depth, through an example of **how to actually DO UDL**.

In our years of UDL work together, I came to know Kendra and Luis as two of the "best modelers of UDL" that I had ever come to know. Here, in this important addition to the field of education, they share their knowledge, experiences, and perspectives so that you can learn to model UDL in your own work. Enjoy your trip into the world of UDL and get ready to **DIVE INTO UDL!**

—Elizabeth M. Dalton, Ph.D.

Introduction

Michael Phelps was not merely a great swimmer; he was also one of the best athletes of all time. At age 18, he won eight medals (six of them gold) at the 2004 Summer Olympics in Athens, Greece. By the time his swimming career had come to an end, Phelps had won twenty-eight medals (twenty-three of them gold), making him the most decorated Olympic athlete in history.

Swimming came easy to the young Michael, but success in the classroom was a different story. An inability to focus was his main challenge, and it would eventually lead to a diagnosis of ADHD around the time he was nine years old. Fortunately for young Michael, his mom was a veteran educator with more than two decades of experience teaching middle school. In many ways, she began to practice some of the principles of Universal Design for Learning (UDL) to help Michael with his learning challenges, even if she did not refer to them by that name. As she put it in an interview for *ADDitude Magazine*, "Whenever a teacher would say 'Michael can't do this,' I'd counter with, 'well, what are you doing to help him?'" (Dutton, 2007). Debbie Phelps clearly understood that with the right supports in place to account for his challenges, her son could learn.

When the young Michael complained about reading, his mom used his interest in sports to keep him engaged. When a math problem stumped him, she would reframe it in a different way until it made sense to him. She might ask him "How long would it take to swim 500 meters if you swim 3 meters per second?" thus relating the problem to his interest in swimming (Dutton, 2007). Years before the development of UDL, Debbie Phelps understood the importance of engagement as a lever that could be used to help learners like her son overcome barriers to learning.

Michael Phelps was lucky his mom was a skilled educator. Not all learners are so lucky. Although all educators can develop the skills of a Debbie Phelps, they often do so through a long process of trial and error. With UDL, the goal is to make this process more intentional. Much of the practice of UDL is what a lot of educators would recognize as "good teaching." UDL is not adding one more thing to educators' already full plates, but building on their best practices by making sure these practices are applied more systematically and with intention. UDL is thus a blueprint for ensuring what we do in the classroom is not just good teaching but *good teaching for everyone, and by design.*

> ***Tweet:*** UDL is a blueprint for ensuring what we do in the classroom is not just "good teaching" but good teaching for everyone, and by design. #DiveIntoUDL

A Quick Definition

The Center for Applied Special Technology (CAST) defines UDL as a framework to improve and optimize teaching and learning *for all people* based on scientific insights into how humans learn (CAST, 2017). That may be a lot to take in if you are just getting started with UDL, but have no fear. In Part 2 of *Dive into UDL*, we will examine the definition more closely as we delve into the many insights from the learning sciences that support the ongoing development and practice of UDL. For now, you just need to know that one of those insights is the great variability that exists among learners. Learners vary in what they find motivating (the *why* of learning), in how they are able to take in and process information in order to make meaning from it (the *what* of learning), and in how they are able to respond in order to demonstrate their understanding (the *how* of learning) (CAST, 2017). They may be strong in one area (remembering the information they read), yet struggle and need support in the others (maintaining their focus or expressing their thoughts). Addressing this variability requires a more flexible approach to instruction that adapts the curriculum to the variable needs of learners, rather than the other way around.

With UDL, this is accomplished by providing learners with options in the form of multiple means of engagement to recruit their interest and drive their motivation for learning, multiple means of representation to make information more accessible and understandable, and multiple means of action and expression to differentiate how learners can express what they know (Meyer, Rose, & Gordon, 2014; CAST 2017) (Figure I.1).

You can see some elements of UDL in how Debbie Phelps adapted the presentation of the math problems to a format that worked better for her son Michael. Debbie recognized that Michael was goal-directed and a hard worker based on his progress in the pool, but just needed information to be presented in a more relatable way to account for his limited attention span. With just a small change in how the information was presented, the frustration Michael experienced when approaching his math assignments was reduced.

Universal Design for Learning
Learners vary...

In what they find motivating.

The **WHY** of learning.

In how they take in, process, and make meaning from information.

The **WHAT** of learning.

In how they are able to demonstrate their learning.

The **HOW** of learning.

Figure I.1 Because learners vary, UDL provides them with options by addressing the why, what, and how of learning in multiple ways.

Developing Expert Learners

Michael Phelps' experience shows that even when we are world class in one area, we can struggle in others. That is the nature of variability. We each have, as Todd Rose has so brilliantly explained in his TEDx Talk "The Myth of Average," a jagged learning profile (TEDx Talks, 2013). We are good at some things (vocabulary, memory, or the ability to swim really fast in Michael's case) but maybe not so good at others (planning, organization, or the ability to focus for Michael). The key to success isn't just shoring up weaknesses while building on strengths. It's about recognizing "strengths" and "weaknesses" are not only internal to the learner, but external to the environment: created or amplified by our instructional design. It's about redefining what learning and success look like, as well as providing multiple pathways to get there. As this book will explore, UDL provides many ways to accomplish this. One way is by creating a learning environment that has the right balance of challenge and support to account for the variability all learners bring into the classroom: finding a variety of ways and means to help each one become an expert learner.

Pause and Reflect

In what ways is your own learning profile "jagged?" What are some areas of learning where you are strong? What are some areas that are more of a challenge for you?

Over the years, some of the techniques Debbie Phelps taught her son Michael became internalized to the point where she no longer had to prompt him as much. In the same *ADDitude Magazine* interview, she explained how she came up with a prompt to calm the young Michael down whenever he became frustrated with his performance in the pool. From the stands, she would form the letter "C" with her hand, which stood for "compose yourself." Later, when she became visibly stressed while juggling several activities at home, Michael flashed her the same C sign that she had used to help him focus in the pool (Dutton, 2007).

That anecdote illustrates both the goal of UDL, helping students become expert learners, as well as the means to help them get there. Through the gradual release of responsibility, learners internalize not only the skills and strategies but their internal motivation as well. They move from being novice learners, who need the support of an external prompt (the C sign for Michael, for instance) to expert ones, who are able to independently recall the strategy for themselves and others (as Michael did for his mother). Novice learners require quite a bit of prompting and support, while expert ones are capable of self-regulating with minimal external intervention. Through practice, they develop a rich repertoire of skills and strategies to help them cope with challenging situations on their own.

UDL aims to create an environment that allows every learner, not just those who have been identified with a disability or "learning difference," to develop into an expert learner. We may not all develop into world-class swimmers, but with the right supports in place we can all definitely get more out of our individual potential, whether it's in swimming, project planning, or learning math.

> **Tweet:** Gradual release of responsibility—Learners internalize skills & strategies AND their motivation, moving from novice to expert learner. #DiveIntoUDL

From Special Education to Universal Design

Although UDL has the development of learning expertise by all learners as its core, many educators still believe that it is only about meeting the needs of learners with special needs. A conversation we had while representing the ISTE Inclusive Learning Network at an ISTE conference a few years ago made this clear. As we explained the mission of our group, one educator responded, "I don't teach special ed." This was a wake up call for us, because it represented two of the most commonly held misconceptions: that there is a group of learners with different needs from most of our "average" students and someone else teaches them; and that UDL and inclusive technology apply only to those students identified within this group.

In fact, the complete opposite is true:

- Every learner has strengths, needs, and preferences.
- UDL is for every one of our learners.

By dispelling the misconceptions surrounding UDL, one of our goals with *Dive into UDL* is to help all educators see the value of UDL as an approach for instructional design and decision-making. We hope to facilitate the much-needed bridge building between general and special educators to ensure that both are benefiting from the best ideas and practices in their respective fields.

The misconceptions surrounding UDL likely have their roots in its history. Originally, UDL began as an attempt to make education more responsive to the needs of learners "in the margins." These were learners who had been left behind in education because they had special needs that could be difficult to address in a traditional classroom environment. UDL came about at a time when technology and learning science were just starting to catch up to changes in public policy. Just a few years earlier in 1975, the first special education law had been passed in the U.S. This was the precursor of what would later be renamed the Individuals with Disabilities Education Act (IDEA). School districts were faced with a new challenge: how to create educational programs that would allow students with disabilities to succeed along with their non-disabled peers.

> *Tweet:* #UDL is not Special Education. UDL is the development of learning expertise by all learners, NOT just meeting the needs of learners with special needs. #DiveIntoUDL

The Center for Applied Special Technology (CAST) originally set out to meet this challenge by developing new technologies that would allow students with disabilities to overcome the barriers they were encountering in the classroom. The idea was to create more flexible alternatives to print, a fixed format that often placed diverse learners who required more customized solutions at a disadvantage. For example, CAST began by developing digital books that included a number of supports for individual learners: text to speech that could read the text aloud for those with reading challenges, glossaries with linked definitions for those with limited vocabulary, large buttons for those with low vision, and single-switch support for those who needed help turning the pages.

Over time, the CAST team came to an important realization: Although these digital books designed for individual learners had a significant impact on the lives of those learners, they did little to remove the systemic barriers. Assumptions and beliefs about learning, and curriculum design were the real problems. The CAST team also realized that the solutions they were developing did not have to be limited to students with identified disabilities. They could benefit all learners if implemented more widely. This shift in thinking and approach was largely inspired by the Universal Design movement in architecture and product design (Chapter 5 discusses this more thoroughly).

The rethinking of UDL as an approach that could meet the needs of all learners was facilitated by developments in both technology and the learning sciences. As you will learn in Chapters 5 and 6, new brain imaging technologies were exposing the myth of the "average learner" as a statistical concept that did not describe actual learners. From a distance the brains of individual learners may look similar, but taking a closer look at the learning brain in action reveals a more complex picture. Even while performing the same task, the patterns of activation vary greatly between learners, a fact that is captured in a popular phrase among UDL practitioners: "our brains are as unique as our fingerprints."

> **Tweet:** The average learner doesn't exist. Design for variability. Our learners' brains are "as unique as their fingerprints." #DiveIntoUDL

UDL and Technology

Fortunately, as our understanding of the learning brain improved and supported the idea of learner variability, a revolution took place in the world of technology. Starting with the personal computer in the 1980s, text-to-speech and speech-to-text software in the 1990s, and the ubiquitous smartphone and tablets appearing around 2009, computing became more accessible to the masses as it became more affordable and easier to use. Today, the smartphone most of us carry in our pockets has more raw computing power than the computer that once took astronauts to the moon. More importantly for us, it also includes a number of built-in accessibility features that can be used to customize the experience for each user: from adjusting the size of the text displayed on the screen to listening to that content with text to speech.

For educators, the challenge now lies in how to harness the power and flexibility offered by emerging technologies to improve learning in a meaningful way. As school districts began to spend significant sums of money on technology acquisition, it became clear that just adding the devices to the classroom was not enough to bring about the desired improvements in student engagement and learning outcomes. It was at that point that a number of frameworks came into play. The two that we will concern ourselves with in this book are the UDL Guidelines (CAST, 2011, 2018), and the ISTE Standards for Students and Educators (International Society for Technology in Education [ISTE], 2016 and 2017). At its core, a framework is a statement of our values. A framework provides a compass to guide our work and ensure it is always aligned with our values. As such, a framework, standard, or guideline is not a checklist. It is more of a *heuristic*: a tool for ongoing reflection and study through which we can examine the curriculum and ensure it reflects our goals and intentions.

> **Tweet:** The UDL guidelines are not a checklist. #UDL is a heuristic tool for ongoing reflection to examine our practice & ensure it reflects our goals & intentions. #DiveIntoUDL

For UDL, the core value is that *everyone deserves the opportunity to become an expert learner* and to reach his or her full potential in a learning environment that is as free of barriers as possible. In order for this goal to be realized, UDL emphasizes the need for flexible instructional design over rigid one-size-fits-all (or, actually, one-size-fits-none) approaches. Although UDL is based on a pedagogy-first stance and can be implemented even in the absence of technology, technology expands the reach and impact of UDL, making it easier to implement on a wide scale. One example would be providing a human reader for a student who struggles with print. At first, this solution appears to be a good UDL solution because it provides another option for that learner to access the content. In practice, however, it would be difficult to implement if several learners in your class required a similar accommodation. Perhaps more importantly, from an engagement perspective, it also reinforces the abled/disabled mindset and forces learners to forego their independence and agency that others take for granted. A more practical (and empowering) solution would be to provide a digital and accessible version of the text so that multiple learners (because of need or preference) can access it independently by having it read to them with a screen reader or text to speech, two options that are now frequently built-in on most personal computers and mobile devices. The latter is a more scalable solution with the potential to impact more learners.

> **Tweet:** Everyone deserves the opportunity to become an expert learner in a learning environment that is as free of barriers as possible. #DiveIntoUDL

Pause and Reflect

Do you think it is possible to implement UDL without technology? If so, what are some of the tradeoffs for learners?

The Design and Organization of the Book

Dive into UDL embodies UDL's emphasis of flexible instructional design over rigid, linear routes to learning goals. Although you may be reading a paper-based copy of this book, our goal isn't a linear experience (Figure I.2). We want to provide you with options and choice in your learning, as well as a variety of means to engage with the information and apply it to your practice. Part of our goal for doing so is to model UDL, but it's also to provide you with an experience of learning similar to what your students experience in their (outside of

Traditional Reading

Figure I.2 The traditional, linear path to reading a book is reading chapter by chapter; "doing something" with the book, such as jotting notes; then putting the book on a shelf—and often forgetting it.

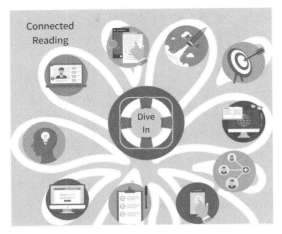

Figure I.3 Connected reading makes learning a personalized digital experience.

school) learning—interconnected digital resources, tools, and communities that allow for a personalized experience: unique to the learner (Figure I.3). We don't expect all of you to move lock step through the book in a linear fashion (although you certainly can do so) and come away with the same standard experience. You can even step away from the pages into the supplemental online environment we created to customize your experience based on needs, strengths, and preferences. Together, the book and online environment embody UDL by including multiple means of engagement, representation, and action and expression for you to find personal meaning in the content. On the companion site (**DiveIntoUDL .com**), you can read a summary of chapters, access interactives to explore ideas, watch videos, find support materials to dive deeper, and explore options to reflect on your practice. The choice is yours!

Ideas from the Field

Beyond the theoretical aspects of UDL we also want to focus on the practical aspects, the "what does this look like and sound like in my classroom?" approach. With this in mind, Part 3 of *Dive into UDL* analyzes a model lesson using a UDL lens. We have also enlisted the support of educators from across North America to share how they redesigned their favorite lessons (or threw a lesson out altogether) to better model and embrace UDL. Their experiences are captured in short interviews on the companion website. We are excited to share their work with you and hope that you will find it exciting and inspiring—so much so that you share your UDL lesson (and journey) with us!

Multiple Entry Points

Based on our experience with professional learning activities we have participated in and developed, we strongly felt this book should have multiple entry points to accommodate the variability educators as adult learners themselves bring to this experience. To accomplish this goal, we designed *Dive into UDL* to be similar to a *Choose Your Own Adventure* novel and align with the principles of UDL. Inspired by the experiences of Michael Phelps as both an athlete and a learner, chapters include a "Wade In" section that addresses a foundational concept, then move to a "Shallow Swim" section that extends and builds upon your previous knowledge of UDL concepts, and finally reach a "Deep Dive" section where you can explore the depths of UDL for your own classroom and as a UDL leader, supporting those who might be at earlier stages of understanding and application. For a more personalized learning experience, you will be able to "start where you are" in your understanding of UDL and grow in that understanding over time with ongoing reflection and application of the concepts to real life problems and situations. (See Chapter 3 for more advice on choosing whether to wade, swim, or dive.) To promote this reflection and help you identify the key ideas presented in each chapter, you will find a number of "Pause and Reflect" prompts throughout the text.

We encourage you to record your thoughts and reflections when you see these prompts. You can do this in any medium: video, journal, sketchnotes, audio, blog, podcast, concept map, and so on. We'll admit, in the past when asked to do this, we've often just thought about it. After all, we're busy and didn't need this additional step. We convinced ourselves we'd just "keep it in our heads." However, research says documenting and revisiting our goals and reflections improves our chances of success. Although you can keep your thoughts to yourself, we found our best insights and learning happened when we recorded our thoughts, reflected on our actions, and shared them with others (and others benefitted too).

We hope your learning about UDL will not stop with this book or even with you. We hope you will consider creating a professional learning community (PLC) or study group with other teachers so that you can support each other as you implement what you learn. By building a community of practice around UDL, you will model the kind of collaborative and supportive environments we want to build in our classrooms for all of our learners.

As you become an expert learner with regard to UDL, we hope you will also come to see yourself as a leader who can support other educators (or pre-service educators) as they apply what they learn to their instructional practice and reflect on their learning in a community with others who are passionate about learners and learning. In this way, UDL will not be a set of static concepts or ideas, or a to-do checklist, but a dynamic and evolving approach that bends to the unique needs of your own educational community.

Pause and Reflect

Consider how you can share your learning. Discussions with colleagues within your school or personal learning community (PLC) are a good beginning, but think beyond these to a wider audience. What about a blog or blog post, videos, tweets, webinars, a Twitter chat, an article, or research? Joining ISTE and our personal learning network (PLN), the Inclusive Learning Network, gave us amazing opportunities to reach out in many ways, including writing this book! If you are unsure how to get started sharing beyond your school, ISTE is a great place to start.

Our Goals for this Book

A key idea of UDL that we want to model is that of being clear on the goals of any instructional activity. With that in mind, here are our goals for this book. We hope to help you:

- Deepen your understanding of the UDL approach and identify areas within your philosophy of teaching and learning that correspond or contrast with this approach.

- Be more intentional in your application of UDL through a better understanding of what UDL is and isn't and how it applies to your particular subjects or areas of instruction.

- Incorporate accessible learning materials and technologies into your instructional design in order to ensure the options and choices you provide learners do not actually result in the erection of new barriers to learning.

- Build more inquiry-based, project-based and constructivist hands-on and minds-on learning opportunities into your UDL lessons in order to engage and inspire learners.

- Apply a gradual release model of instruction to help learners move from the role of dependent, externally motivated learners to independent, intrinsically motivated expert learners.

- Expand and enhance your current instructional practices by applying a UDL lens to deconstruct (and rebuild) existing lessons so that they incorporate UDL principles.

- Engage in a cycle of continuous professional growth through job-embedded inquiry based on lesson plan deconstruction, design, implementation, and reflection.

Pause and Reflect

After reviewing our list of goals, pick the three that are most important to you. Of these three, which one goal, if you were to accomplish it in the next year, would have the most impact on your professional practice?

Do you have any other personal or professional goals related to the topic of UDL that you would like to pursue?

Those are our goals for this book, but one important idea of UDL is that learning needs to be personalized if it is to be authentic, meaningful, and relevant. To that end, we want you to take a moment to reflect on your own personal goals for picking up and working through this book.

Next Steps—Take Your Mark!

Just like a swimmer, before you can "take your mark" and dive into the pool of learning, you need to invest time in personal assessment, practice, and review. Most of us, regardless of our innate talent, can always improve if we have a meaningful challenge and receive appropriate support. Learning should be more like coaching—for both the student and the teacher. When we find a great coach and have opportunities for positive practice and discussion with others, we can often push ourselves that much further, faster.

Interestingly the ISTE Standards for Educators also promote this approach (Krueger, 2017):

- Start where you are, get out of your comfort zone, and progress at your own pace.
- Practice with others to move towards mastery.
- Don't forget to breathe!

As is the case with an elite athlete like Michael Phelps, change takes time and will often happen in small, incremental steps. The first steps in the journey, whether you are trying to improve your swim times or learn how to implement UDL, are to give yourself permission to try the new approach, take stock of where you are currently, and select the appropriate tools for the task at hand. In the next chapter, we introduce you to two scaffolds or supports that can help in the early stages of your UDL journey: the ISTE Standards for Educators and the UDL Guidelines.

Additional Resources

Throughout the book, you will find Quick Response (QR) codes for accessing additional information in the form of videos and other digital resources available on the book's companion website, **DiveIntoUDL.com**. We placed these codes at the end of each chapter so as not to interrupt the flow of your reading. (Our favorite app for scanning QR codes is 3GVision's i-nigma, which is available for iOS and Android.) Before proceeding to the next chapter, take a minute and give scanning this QR code a try to access the online resources for this introduction.

Website Activities

PART

1

Your Professional Self

Taking Ownership of (Professional) Learning

How do you go about changing your practice to bring in new methods and mindsets? For many of us, this has traditionally been through some type of professional development (PD): an event, led by an expert in the topic. This type of PD is outside our locus of control. We attend, take part, but we don't own it. If we want students to experience a different type of learning—one that is student-driven, inquiry-based, and technology-infused—then we as educators need to experience something similar in our own professional learning (Figure 1.1). Like students, we need to take charge of our own learning, be willing to experiment, ask questions, and use technology to help us solve problems. In short, we need to start seeing ourselves as learners who are on a similar journey of personal growth and agency as our students. How to do this, and where to find support to accelerate your learning is what this chapter is all about.

Figure 1.1 Professional learning needs to mirror what we want to see in the classroom.

Permission to Take Charge of Change

We recognize that change in education is slow. Much of the original industrial model that defines our classrooms remains intact. The focus on standardization and uniformity—for students and educators—is the antithesis of the often-messy process associated with change, and it essentially blocks the adoption of personalized learning approaches, such as UDL. You may face resistance from other educators or your administration when you try to make changes to your practice or to take full ownership of your professional learning. It is tempting to stay with the status quo, especially when you may feel alone in your desire for change. To support you, consider the ISTE Standards for Students (2016), ISTE Standards for Educators (2017), and the UDL Guidelines as valuable tools in your quest to learn and change. You can use them to envision the future and guide your professional growth as you set goals for yourself and your students.

> *Tweet:* Consider #ISTEStandards and #UDL Guidelines as exemplars of what needs to change, as well as valuable tools to guide, support, and accelerate that change. #DiveIntoUDL

The ISTE Standards for Educators (2017) signal and support the big changes that lie ahead. In fact, you can consider them *permission to change*—not only what happens in your classroom or school, but also how you approach and direct your own professional learning.

Covered in depth in Chapter 6, the UDL Guidelines (CAST, 2011, 2017) signal and support the big ideas that underlie the changes ahead. Consider them a *framework for change*. At their core, the Guidelines focus on the creation of equitable and inclusive learning environments. With this base, the Guidelines then provide options to support the *gradual release of responsibility* of learning to students, helping them become expert learners, vital if they are to take on the new roles outlined in the ISTE Standards for Students (2016).

What's New in the ISTE Standards

While recognizing that technology tools and skills are still important, the new ISTE Standards for Students (2016) and for Educators (2017) focus on complex, interconnected roles, signaling a profound change in traditional student-teacher relationships, learning, and the learning environment. The Standards for Educators are composed of seven distinct roles, which are divided into two categories. The Empowered Professional category contains the Learner, Leader, and Citizen roles; while Learning Catalyst contains the Collaborator, Designer, Facilitator, and Analyst roles (Figure 1.2). Not only do the Educator Standards (ISTE, 2017) recognize educators as professionals with an important role to play, they also embed principles of UDL within each role. For the first time, for instance, they explicitly mention learner variability as a key consideration for the design of innovative learning environments. Specifically, Standard 5, Designer, encourages educators to be learning catalysts who can "design authentic, learner-driven activities and environments that recognize and accommodate learner variability," the same concept that is at the core of UDL.

The recognition of learner variability in the new ISTE Standards for Educators (2017) is an exciting and important development. It provides an opportunity for some of the underlying values and concepts of UDL to reach the general educators who most need to know about them in order to support increasingly diverse student populations. By embedding and referencing UDL principles and strategies throughout, the Educator Standards recognize the value of creating more equitable learning opportunities for all learners. For UDL, the ISTE Standards for Educators provide an opportunity to bring technology innovations back into UDL. Embracing the best that new technologies have to offer is one way to make UDL even more relevant for the future.

ISTE Standards for Educators

Figure 1.2 The ISTE Standards for Educators both outline and drive two fundamental shifts in education: technology's role in learning and ownership of learning.

Tweet: The ISTE Standards for Educators provide an opportunity for every educator to use technology innovations to embrace #UDL. #DiveIntoUDL

Three important points about the ISTE Standards align with the design and intent of this book and deserve a closer look.

The first is the choice to lead off both the Student (ISTE, 2016) and Educator (ISTE, 2017) Standards with the role of Learner, emphasizing student agency and educator professionalism. Learner expertise, the goal of UDL, is clearly evident within this (and the remaining) standards. As

Empowered Learners, students are encouraged to set goals, seek feedback, understand their learning needs, customize their learning environment, and build global networks to support their learning. This connects with the UDL goal of helping learners develop into "individuals who are expert at learning—individuals who know how to learn, who have already learned a great deal, and who are eager to learn more" (Meyer, Rose, & Gordon, 2014, p. 84). As *Learners*, educators are also encouraged to set professional learning goals, explore pedagogical ideas deeply and apply them to the classroom, reflect on their practice, and actively participate and learn with other educators globally.

Leading with Learner, the ISTE Standards for Educators (2017) emphasize ownership of learning and highlight the need for fundamental changes to how we currently teach students and support teachers. This significantly changes the purpose (and perhaps identity) of many educators as we move away from the role of teacher to that of *co-learner* with our students.

The second point of interest for us is the division of the Educator Standards (ISTE, 2017) into two categories: Empowered Professional and Learning Catalyst. The term *Empowered Professional* suggests that we have both permission and an obligation to be agents of change: to ask questions, seek answers, and change practice. And in so doing, explicitly model for our learners the skills and dispositions we want them to develop. The second term, *Learning Catalyst*, supports this role, emphasizing the work we do as professionals—collaborating, designing, facilitating, and analyzing—to intentionally create learning environments that meet the needs of all learners.

> **Tweet:** Empowered Professional-ISTE Standards are both permission and an obligation to be agents of change. So ask questions, seek answers & change your practice. #DiveIntoUDL

Lastly, while students are described as empowered, innovative, and creative in the Student Standards (ISTE, 2016), educators have no such descriptions in their standards. This suggests that we can personalize our roles and assume the tasks in ways that support our variability, experience, and expertise. In other words, the Educator Standards (ISTE, 2017) assume our professionalism and give us voice and choice in how we approach the important work we have to do. We can add our own adjectives, changing them as our needs and interests evolve.

> **Tweet:** UDL and ISTE Standards for Educators assume our professionalism & give us voice & choice in how we approach the important work we do @isteconnects. #DiveIntoUDL

Pause and Reflect

Take a moment to review the ISTE Standards for Educators (2017) (**www .iste.org/standards/for-educators**) including the dropdown indicators.

- Where do you feel your teaching practice aligns with the Educator Standards, and where do you need to grow?
- In what ways are you a learner with your students?
- In what ways are you a learner as a professional?
- How do you currently give students ownership of their learning?
- In what ways do you take ownership of your professional learning?
- What adjectives can you add to help you define your roles as Learner, Leader, Citizen, Collaborator, Designer, Facilitator, and Analyst?
- How can you use or reference the Educator Standards to begin a dialogue with colleagues and administration in your school?

Choose Your Own Learning Path

For many of us, our professional options are more like a basal reader—short, controlled, and chosen for us—than a *Choose Your Own Adventure* book with multiple options at key points for us to choose how the story unfolds. Our administration or district plans the PD, and we attend. We may have the option to choose from a menu of sessions, but we are rarely afforded the choice to drive our own professional learning.

The expectation is that educators will learn a theory, methodology, skill, or technology in a setting outside the classroom, usually in a workshop or course led by an expert, and then immediately (and expertly) apply what we learned in the classroom. The irony of this approach seems lost on the designers and presenters. To change practice in significant ways requires the *classroom* to become the location for our professional learning: It must be job-embedded. The day-in and day-out exploration of what works and why rarely happens in a PD event. It happens with our students in our classrooms and is refined through sharing and discussion with our colleagues.

The challenge of embracing this approach is that iterative inquiry processes are inherently messy. This can make people feel uncomfortable, especially as it involves students who must take high stakes tests, and who have parents that worry about their future. In fact, if we "fail" it is often looked on negatively by parents, administrators, and even ourselves. Traditional PD, documented through seat time or PD hours, is straightforward to administer, track, and quantify. It's also a rather painless way to avoid change and maintain the status quo (Cole, 2004). An example of this is an online course Kendra took on constructivism. Participants worked alone on assignments, had prescribed readings for each week, and did obligatory posts in response to questions. The affordance of technology (and the irony) was lost on the professor. Imagine if participants had co-created the course and then applied the principles learned to their classroom environment, rather than replicate what already exists?

Tweet: "Do as I say, not as I do" needs to stop. Professional learning needs to mirror the #collaborative, #iterative #inquiry process we want to see in our classrooms. #DiveIntoUDL

Perhaps you've been attending PD for years and you've enjoyed it. There is nothing inherently wrong with PD. It is often necessary, such as when you need to learn your school's new learning management system (LMS), but insufficient. On its own, it rarely brings about deep and sustained change. Despite decades of professional development, one study found that "teachers changed little in terms of the content they teach, the pedagogy they use to teach it, and their emphasis on performance goals for students" (as quoted in Timperley, Wilson, Barrar, & Fung, 2007). There are many reasons for this. People are creatures of habit. They often resist change, or they need a good reason to make the change. It can also be scary to change and risk failure in a public venue, such as a classroom. Luckily, more research and thought leaders are endorsing new ways of teaching and learning. The tide is turning.

Think of it as learning to swim. Publically flailing your arms and swallowing what feels like gallons of water can be embarrassing and frightening. The safest place is to remain in the shallow end of the pool. It takes courage to learn to swim, to venture into the deep end, and be observed by and dependent on others to help you learn to swim. However, when we risk failure, we not only learn to swim, but we also model for our students the effort, courage, and mindset we want to see in them. It's time to take the plunge. Jump in, the water's fine!

Pause and Reflect

We've all probably attended, and maybe even led, a professional development (PD) session like Kendra's online course (full disclosure: we have). Take a moment to consider the PD you've experienced—the good and not so good. Ask yourself:

- Is this type of PD needed? When is it appropriate? What does it reinforce?
- What might need to happen before? After?
- What PD have you attended that positively impacted your instruction and why?
- What PD have you attended that did little to change your instruction and why?

Next Steps

This chapter has been all about setting the stage for the changes in your practice that lie ahead as you implement UDL in your classroom. With the Educator Standards (ISTE, 2017) providing *permission to change* and try out new approaches, the UDL Guidelines nicely intersect with them, serving as the *framework for that change*. One way to jumpstart change is by rethinking the relationship between educators and students, so that they come to see each other as co-learners and co-designers of learning experiences built around UDL. This transformation in roles and responsibilities starts with a different approach to how educators themselves learn, which is the focus of the next chapter.

Website Activities

Before moving to the next chapter, we encourage you to scan the QR code to access the book's companion website where you can extend your learning with additional resources.

Professional Development versus Professional Learning

The term *professional learning* is often used interchangeably with the phrase *professional development*, but it shouldn't be. So, what is the difference?

Professional Development

Professional development (PD) is often offered or mandated by administration. Someone at a school or district level determines staff needs and creates PD to support it. It most often takes the form of a motivational speaker, expert, or specialist who leads a presentation, workshop, or event. More and more it happens online with little change to the structure or design of the learning.

PD can be viewed as a noun. It's an event you attend. It can be informative, boring, inspiring, irrelevant, active, or passive. Regardless of how (or how well) PD is delivered, there is little evidence to suggest that the enormous amount of time and money spent on PD has resulted in systemic change to instructional practice or large gains in student achievement.

> "Professional development involves workshops, courses, programs, and related activities that are designed presumably to provide teachers with new ideas, skills, and competencies necessary for improvement in the classroom. The notion that external ideas alone will result in changes in the classroom and school is deeply flawed as a theory of action. I am not only referring to irrelevant or poorly conducted professional development, but also to sessions that meet the highest standard of adult learning." (Fullan, 2007)

This doesn't mean that PD doesn't have value. It does. However, it is only one small part of the learning process for educators, as you'll see in just a moment.

Professional Learning

Professional learning is the "application of an iterative cycle of inquiry that teachers engage in daily, within a collaborative and supportive environment; with the intent to change practice" (Hannay, Wideman, & Seller, 2006). This type of professional learning isn't an event or even a series of events. It is behavior, a behavior shared with others.

It is interesting to us just how similar the process of professional learning is to the type of learning we want to happen in our classrooms: social, collaborative, co-constructed, inquiry-based, and reflective. It closely matches the ISTE Standards for Students (2016) and, of course, learner expertise as defined by UDL.

> "In practice, inquiry engages teachers as learners in critical and creative thinking. It honours openness and flexibility. Through collaborative dialogue, teachers seek emergent possibilities—new questions and solutions to student learning and achievement. This stance is 'iterative,' repeating progressively as teachers reflect and build on each successive inquiry." (Ontario Ministry of Education, 2010)

So to recap, professional learning isn't a noun. It isn't an event or even a series of events. It is a process, and a habit. Professional learning happens in the classroom, defined and refined through reflection and discussion with others. Professional learning is a verb.

A bit overwhelmed? No worries. Let's bring professional learning back to our analogy. These changes to your practice don't need to be a marathon swim. You can venture into the water a little bit each day: perfecting your stroke one day, swimming a bit longer the next. Incremental change is better than floundering in the deep end. And, just like swimming, it's always safer and more pleasant to swim with others.

⏸ *Pause and Reflect*

- How does your school or district support your professional growth?
- How would you define the difference between professional development and professional learning?
- As an educator, what is the single biggest thing you've changed about your teaching in the last two or three years? How did the change come about?
- Do you have a professional growth plan?
- Do you regularly reflect on your teaching practice? Alone? With others?

Tweet: PD is often an event determined by the district, led by an expert. Professional learning, by contrast, is a process and a habit. It happens in the classroom and is refined through reflection and discussion with other educators. #DiveIntoUDL

Professional Growth

Now, you may ask, "What about PD and conferences and other events? Do we just ignore them or fight them?" Definitely not. As we mentioned, we don't believe PD is wrong; it just isn't enough.

Let's take a closer look at all the elements that can support your professional growth, as diagramed in Figure 2.1. At the center is professional learning: the investigative process teachers engage in on a daily basis that we described in the last section. The Inquire, Plan, Act, Reflect cycle (IPAR) is just one possible process. Your district may have its own, or you may use one like Linda Kaser and Judy Halbert's Spiral of Inquiry (**bit.ly/DiveIntoUDLCh2a**). Or you may find some that embed themselves in the larger co-learner community context, such as Learning Forward's Cycle of Continuous Improvement (**bit.ly/DiveIntoUDLCh2b**) or Insight Education Group's Supporting Teacher Effectiveness Program (**bit.ly/DiveIntoUDLCh2c**).

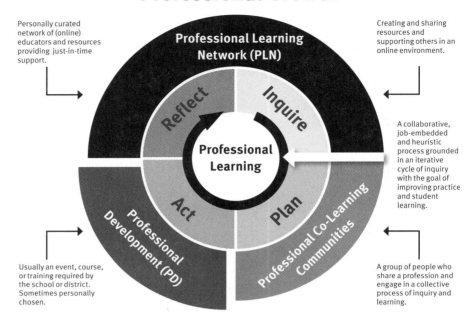

Figure 2.1 Professional growth is a blend of professional learning, an iterative inquiry process practiced daily, aligned with and supported by your professional networks, communities, and development.

Whatever process guides your professional learning, look for these key components:

- **Ongoing, cyclical**: Questions are asked, implemented, and reflected upon, which results in new questions to be explored
- **Heuristic**: Hands-on, experiential, in the classroom, with the students
- **Connected to daily practice**: Questions to investigate are applicable to the learning that happens in the classroom and can be explored there
- **Flexible, just-in-time**: Options to personalize resources, support available to fit needs and preferences
- **Collaborative**: Educators come together to reflect on their practice, recognizing that change happens over time, together

- **Technology-supported**: Includes technology both as a means to connect to other educators and as a tool embedded in teaching and learning

Surrounding and supporting this iterative process are three interrelated components:

- **Professional learning network** (**PLN**): A personally curated network of (mostly online) educators and resources providing just-in-time support for your professional growth. When you are ready, it includes the reciprocal process of you creating and sharing resources and supporting others in these environments.

- **Professional co-learning communities** (**PCC**): A group of people who share a profession and engage in a collective process of inquiry and learning. This could be within your school, within your district, or online. In the best of all possible worlds, it isn't a requirement but a choice to participate with other professionals.

- **Professional development** (**PD**): Usually an event, course, or training required by the school or district and sometimes personally chosen from a menu of options. It can support professional learning when it aligns with the attainment of knowledge and skills that support your professional learning goals.

While you don't have to engage in all three areas at once, consider how each component supports your professional learning over time. You'll notice that there is definite overlap between each category, and that is just fine. Don't get hung up on whether something is part of your PLN or PD. It could be both. Try to maintain a balance and, more importantly, ownership. Some are more personalized and flexible, others are more formal and organized. Some let you connect with like-minded educators (PLN), others may stretch your thinking (PCC). All should support your professional learning.

Figure 2.2 Professional learning shouldn't put you to sleep. It should empower you.

The work we do as teachers is very public. Everyone has an opinion about what works in education. And it seems, everyone has a suggestion for what we need to do next. While it is important as a nation, state, district, and school to be aligned in our goals, we suggest it's important for you to choose your own professional learning path, resist the one-size-fits-all PD sessions, and engage in professional learning that leaves you feeling empowered, not sleepy (Figure 2.2).

"But wait!" You may be thinking, "My administrator (or district or professor) wants me to read this book! Isn't this just PD in disguise?" We hope not! Our goal is for this book to be used as a heuristic tool to help you start and sustain your own professional growth—with others.

Next Steps

In the UDL classroom, the relationship between the teacher and the students changes as the responsibility for learning is gradually transferred to learners who are developing their learning expertise. The traditional way many educators learn, through PD, does not adequately model this transfer of responsibility. Instead, the provider of the PD, as a stand-in for the classroom teacher, models the sage-on-the-stage approach to learning. In this chapter, we have encouraged you to rethink how you approach your own learning as a more iterative and reflective process that is the embodiment of a verb rather than a noun. A key element of that process is a sense of control and ownership of your own learning. Model the kind of self-determined learning you will promote as you implement UDL with your students. In the next chapter, you will have an opportunity to exert that kind of control as you determine your starting point for learning about UDL and the depth of discussion that best meets your needs. Before you continue, use the QR code to access additional information, videos, activities, and interactives on the companion website.

Website Activities

What's Your Zone?

We all bring different levels of ability, experience, and interest to the task of learning. As educators, we need to allow ourselves to be learners, at different levels, and model the love of lifelong learning we want to see in our students. One way to do this is by actively engaging in professional learning, sharing what you know with your peers, while gaining new knowledge from them. In this chapter, we'll also help you identify your starting level of knowledge with UDL, so you can choose your best path to learning more.

Find Your Peeps

Think back to your best learning as professionals. For us, the courses and papers we co-created with other professional educators, our work with K–20 educators in the ISTE Inclusive Learning Network, and preparing presentations for the annual ISTE conference (PD) immediately came to mind. Books, events, PD, and social media, however, provide only the content and location for our learning. Much of our professional growth can be attributed to the *social construction* of our learning. As we plan, design, and present with our peers, each of us steps up to support others' learning, and in turn are supported by others when we needed it. We experience a sense of a rotating More Knowledgeable Other (MKO) (Vygotsky, 1978), which creates a synergy, where we create and learn, beyond what we could achieve alone. Although some of that can happen with peers face-to-face, the connections can be virtual, as well.

As an adult learner, reaching out to others in online spaces can deepen and extend your Zone of Proximal Development, or ZPD (Vygotsky, 1978), which is the space between what is known and unknown, the space between

Figure 3.1 With the support of your colleagues in your professional Zone of Proximal Development your learning can take off.

what you can and cannot do, and, most importantly, the space where learning occurs (Figure 3.1). On your own you can continue to learn and grow, but within your professional ZPD, with the help of your peers, you will be able to go further and faster. You will have resources and support where and when you need it. But more importantly, you will be able to start where you are in your understanding, then share your learning and reflections, knowing others are there to support you, and help you out when needed. Not only do these trusted colleagues, your peeps, have your back, they can also push you to do more!

How can you build and extend your professional ZPD for UDL? Going forward consider us your UDL peeps! Reach out and connect with us on Twitter at #DiveIntoUDL. You've just expanded your professional ZPD! Together we truly are learning catalysts.

> **Tweet:** Expand your professional ZPD. On your own you can continue to learn and grow, but with the help of your peers, you will be able to go farther and faster. These trusted colleagues, your peeps, have your back, and can push you to do more! Consider us your #UDL peeps. #DiveIntoUDL

Find Where You Are

When we introduce the term *UDL* to educators, we sometimes hear "I'm already doing that" or "It's just good teaching." Although it's true that good teachers often include aspects of UDL in their practices, UDL isn't just good teaching. It's the intentional application of UDL principles to your practice, challenging what you currently think and do, so that all learners can succeed.

We know, from personal experience, there is always something new about UDL to discover and apply to our practices. Our knowledge and skills grow as we work, reflect, and share with other educators. At the same time, you may already know a lot about UDL, even if you don't identify what you are doing as such. An assessment can help you identify the gaps in your understanding so that you can choose the best path for addressing them in Part 2 of the book.

Assessment Does Not Equal Evaluation

With an "always learning" attitude in mind, the next step is to take an assessment. The goal is to help you better gauge your current understanding of UDL, so you can build on your understanding. Scan the QR code in the margin or visit **DiveIntoUDL.com** to complete the UDL assessment.

UDL Knowledge Assessment

Do assessments make you nervous? Formative assessment or assessment for learning (AfL) shouldn't. Both you and your students should look at formative assessment as an opportunity to grow by assessing what you know and what you don't know—yet. Remember this isn't a test but a snapshot; it isn't evaluative or punitive in its intent. The results will help you to personalize your use of this book, as well as support and guide your professional learning journey. The goal isn't to become an expert in UDL today, but to slowly add elements of UDL into your instructional practice, observe their effect on learners and learning, reflect on and share what you learned, and then add another element to increase your understanding and skills over time.

Individual Medley

Think back to the swimming analogy. You may be a good swimmer, but to complete the individual medley you need to master four strokes: butterfly, backstroke, breaststroke, and freestyle. It isn't going to happen overnight. You may be already proficient in one area but struggle with another. It takes practice, and in the beginning, conscious effort to master each stroke. UDL is the same. Trying to understand all facets of the UDL Guidelines and their three principles—Engagement, Representation, and Action and Expression—or to change your instructional practice too quickly could result in your just skimming the surface or sinking below it. Slow down. Stop, plan, and take a breather to keep your goal in sight.

You may be unfamiliar with UDL. By choosing your path, you'll soon know more about UDL and be able to apply it successfully to your classroom teaching. On the other end of the spectrum, perhaps you're an expert in UDL. This book will help you refine your understanding and help you support others in your school, district, or online community to grow their UDL practices.

Next Steps

Now that you've assessed your level of understanding, you can use your tally as a guide to determine how deep a dive you'll take into UDL. Depending on your starting level of knowledge, you may start by wading

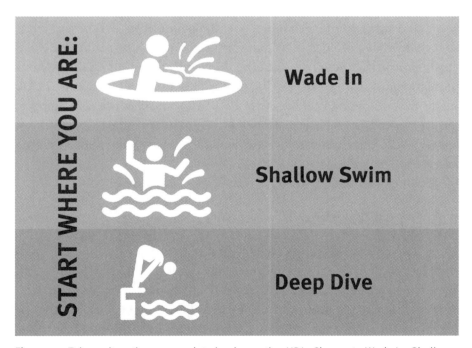

Figure 3.2 Take an iterative approach to implementing UDL: Choose to Wade In, Shallow Swim, or Deep Dive. *Icons by Freepik from flaticon.com*

in to test the water. When you're ready, you can take a short swim in the shallow end where you are still able to stand up to get your bearings or take a quick rest before diving in again. Finally, when you're more confident, you can dive into the deep end, with the reassurance that life jackets and other swimmers (your colleagues and us!) are right there with you to help you stay afloat.

Throughout the remainder of *Dive into UDL*, you'll be presented with options and choice to explore topics in ways that meet your needs as a learner as you increase your understanding and application of UDL. To help you spot which sections and chapters meet your needs, we've identified them by the three knowledge levels illustrated in Figure 3.2.

Wade In: This is new to me. I am unfamiliar or only vaguely familiar with the term, concept, or idea and would like to learn more.

Shallow Swim: I have heard of this and understand some aspects. I'm ready to learn more. I still have some questions and want to continue to improve my practice in this area.

Deep Dive: I feel confident in my understanding and want to expand my knowledge and refine my practice. I would like to support others in this area.

In the next chapter, look for the section marked with the icon that fits your knowledge level and skip ahead to it if you like. Remember, you have options and choice in how you learn—and read! In addition, you can scan the QR code to find additional activities, videos, and other digital resources on the companion website.

Website Activities

PART 2

UDL and You

Your Assumptions and Beliefs

The classroom is an extremely busy place with dozens of moving parts, dozens of personalities, and hundreds of demands on our time in any given day. There are just too many pieces of information for us to process or even notice them all. In many ways, the classroom is an example of the *selective attention principle* (Simons, 2010) at work. The effects of selected attention are illustrated in Daniel Simons and Christopher Chabris's famous "Gorilla" video (**bit.ly/DiveIntoUDLCh4a**): When instructed to count the number of times the players in white pass a basketball during the video, viewers become so focused on the passes that they fail to see a person in a gorilla suit walk through the game.

Our focus becomes a filter.

For many of us, our assumptions and beliefs about learning and learners become our focus and our filter. We expect to see certain behaviors: for certain students to succeed, for other students to struggle. We count the passes, but counting the passes reinforces our expectations so we fail to see the gorilla walk across the floor.

It's only when we consciously look for the gorilla—when someone points out that we *should* look for the gorilla—that we see it. If you are lucky enough to have experienced the Simons and Chabris video without prior knowledge of its intent, it is an eye-opening moment. You can't believe you missed the gorilla. It's so obvious! However, some will insist the video was doctored. There is no way they missed that gorilla! The gorilla wasn't there. If you want to give the test another try, take a look at "The Monkey Business Illusion" (**bit.ly/DiveIntoUDLCh4c**) or "Movie Perception Test" (**bit.ly/DiveIntoUDLCh4b**), which illustrate the same concept.

What's the "gorilla moment" in your professional life? It's when what you *expect* to see and pay attention to causes you to miss or misinterpret something important. It might be observing your class engaged in a task and missing the student quietly struggling. It might be watching a student not know what to do next and assuming they weren't listening to your instructions. It could be assigning leveled text based on learners' decoding skills, rather than their excellent comprehension skills when using a screen reader.

For Kendra, the gorilla moment was assuming disability was internal to the student and not dependent on a variety of factors within her control to change. She saw learners struggling with reading and writing tasks and provided technology to accommodate the disability. Although this recognized the underlying ability of the learners, she didn't challenge (until later) the system belief that students who didn't fit the "norm" required a diagnosis and label to get extra support and remediation, or the conventional belief that text-based instruction and assessment were the best ways to teach and for students to learn.

> *Tweet:* What we measure and count is our focus. Our focus then becomes our filter, reinforcing what we "know" about our students. With this laser focus we often miss the gorilla in the room. What's your gorilla? **bit.ly/DiveIntoUDLCh4a** #DiveIntoUDL

Examining your assumptions and beliefs on a regular basis can help you clear your filter. Taking a step back from your teaching to look for the gorilla in your instruction and assessment, the learning environment, or your expectations of students, however, can cause disequilibrium. It can be shocking to suddenly see the gorilla. This is why it is helpful to share and reflect with others. Do they see the gorilla too?

Exploring your assumptions and beliefs about teaching, learning, and learners before you begin exploring more about UDL will give you a benchmark to help you see your professional growth over time. Remember, there are no right or wrong answers to the "Pause and Reflect" questions. This information is for you and your professional growth, so consider recording it in some way to reference later.

⏸ *Pause and Reflect*

Do you see the gorilla?

- How has your understanding of the average student influenced your teaching practice?
- How has your role as a general education or special education teacher shaped your teaching practice?
- Is it possible to reach and teach every student given the vast diversity of learners in our classroom?
- What does it mean to have a disability? Who should support students with disabilities or other learning differences?
- What role does technology play in your life? What role does technology play in your classroom?
- Who currently succeeds in your classroom and why? Did you succeed in the education system? Why or why not?
- What is your role as a teacher? What is the role of a student? What is the goal of learning?

Exploring Your Assumptions and Beliefs

Your assumptions and beliefs are like the clothes in your closet. Some fit perfectly. Some don't fit anymore, but still you hang on to them in case they fit again (they usually don't). Some are old, worn-out favorites that *may* be worth keeping. Can they be updated and repaired, or should they be replaced with something more up-to-date? Some might be trendy. Even if these seem to fit, do they stand up to everyday wear? Will they be replaced when the next trend comes along, or does this trend have its roots in solid design?

Just like performing a seasonal closet clear-out, regularly bring your assumptions and beliefs about learners and learning out into the light and examine them closely (Figure 4.1). Try them on. Be critical. Consider getting a new perspective from your trusted peers during this process, especially those with a critical eye and unflinching honesty!

Figure 4.1 Assumptions and beliefs: Clean out your instructional closet regularly.

Tweet: Regularly "clean" your instructional closet. Review your assumptions and beliefs about learners and learning. Keep what fits, then tailor or dispose of those that no longer do. #DiveIntoUDL

Every teacher comes to teaching with assumptions and beliefs that come from a variety of places and times: our school experiences, our children's (or friend's children's) school experiences, our pre-service, our graduate degrees, the PLN we curate, and the climate and culture of the schools and districts we work in. Some of these assumptions and beliefs may be accurate. Some may be accurate but difficult to implement for a variety of reasons. Others may need updating, refining, or changing. For example, when Luis first started learning about UDL, his focus was primarily on removing barriers by ensuring educational materials were accessible. This focus was shaped by his experience as a legally blind student who experienced frustration in trying to access the information he needed to complete his graduate education. Similarly, when UDL originated at the Center for Applied Special Technology (CAST), the focus was on removing barriers that kept "learners in the margins" (like Luis) from accessing learning. As UDL evolved, this focus expanded to more effectively address the needs of all learners, not just those with identified disabilities.

Kendra came to teaching with the assumption that disabilities were internal to the student, based on a medical model of identifying and labeling students who didn't fit the system. She most likely internalized this message from her schooling as well, because there was little talk about the system not fitting the students. Assistive technology, such as text to speech and speech to text, appeared to be the perfect retrofit for these students. Kendra's "how did I miss that?" moment came while creating a UDL video with Mindy Johnson, a UDL specialist at CAST. In the video, Mindy explained that learner ability (or disability) is at the intersection where the individual and the environment or context met. Kendra suddenly saw what she'd missed: It isn't enough to just provide "disabled" students with technology to "level the playing field." Equally important is changing our instructional practice to better support the variability of our learners. Rather than berate herself for focusing on one aspect of UDL, accessibility, Kendra recognized her understanding and application of UDL had grown and would continue to grow over time.

Rather than take an all or nothing approach, give yourself permission to "start where you are," connect and scaffold to what you already know and do, and then move forward in a purposeful way. The challenge for us as educators is to remain open to examining our beliefs about learners and learning on a regular basis. We must question what we "know" and actively seek evidence that can confirm or refute our assumptions and beliefs (Figure 4.2). By sharing and discussing our assumptions and beliefs with others, we bring them out into the light to examine critically with the defining question: Is this best for *all* our learners?

Figure 4.2 Our current focus on time (number of hours per day, number of periods in a course, number of months in a grade) makes assumptions about learning. Ask yourself: Is time-based learning best for *all* learners?

The next sections explore assumptions and beliefs: Where they come from, how the current system can go against them, and how, when you're ready, you can support others in examining their own. This is your first opportunity to choose your level. Consider your UDL Assessment score from Chapter 3, as well as your experience examining your assumptions and beliefs to help you start where you are:

- **Wade In: The Game of School** (page 30). In this section, you'll consider if you played the *game of school* and how your school experience influences your current assumptions and beliefs.

- **Shallow Swim: System Assumptions and Beliefs** (page 33). In this section, you'll examine how assumptions and beliefs embedded within education impact learners and limit change.

You'll also explore, in detail, the system's assumptions and beliefs about assessment and their far-reaching effects on learning and learners.

- **Deep Dive: Leading the Change** (page 37). In this section, you'll explore how to leverage the ISTE Standards for Educators (2017) to frame the changing role of the educator, as well as discussion points with which to support others as they examine and update their assumptions and beliefs.

Wade In: The Game of School

When first examining your assumptions and beliefs, it is important to reflect on your experience of school. What was it like for you? Were you able to successfully navigate the rules and requirements, or did you struggle? Chances are we all had some bumps in the road, but generally speaking most teachers quickly learned to play the *game of school* when they were students. As education innovator and author A. J. Juliani noted in his blog post "The Game of School vs. The Game of Life," even young students can be adept at playing the game. At age 7 his daughter already knew the rules: "Make the adults at school happy, and the adults at home will be happy" (Juliani, 2017). Students who figure out the rules of the game are usually the most successful in the current system. They are compliant; they listen quietly, put their hands up, stay in their seats, do what they are told, and complete (mainly written) tasks on time and as assigned. Ultimately, in many schools, these are the students who we plan for and teach to.

Whether we realize it or not, many of us may have pursued a career in teaching because we learned to play the game well. We navigated the requirements and avoided most labels. We could completely fulfill the

> *Tweet:* "Good" students play the game of school. They are compliant. They do what they are told. They complete (mainly written) tasks on time and as assigned. Ultimately, in many schools, these are the students who we plan for and teach to. #DiveIntoUDL @ajjuliani

> **Tweet:** UDL shifts the focus to mastering learning, not the game of school. #DiveIntoUDL

reading, writing, and test-taking requirements. We knew the rules and were able to play effectively enough to complete the game and get our degrees. In other words, we represent the subset of students that are successful in the current system.

Kendra's Game of School

Kendra played the game of school—eventually. As she explained:

> "In elementary school I liked to move a lot, and I was very opinionated. Girls in particular were supposed to be quiet and stay in their seats and do their work. I didn't fit this description. I loved to read and write, and I had a good memory. So even though I didn't fit the mold, I was successful. Eventually, I learned to behave like I was supposed to. I developed visual strategies to organize and plan. I learned to keep my opinions to myself—for the most part. My experience, while not devastating, suppressed my authentic self. Although I learned, I'm not sure I learned deeply. Today I might be labeled with ADHD or difficulties with executive functions. (Is it any wonder I worked in special education?)

> "Because I learned differently, I have always sought ways to level the playing field through the application of UDL and technology to my teaching practice. My goal is to help every learner recognize and celebrate their strengths rather than feel less for not fitting the norm."

Luis's Game of School

In fifth grade, Luis's teacher gave an assignment that required the class to memorize the capitals of all the Latin American countries, the kind of rote memorization that defined much of education at that time in the

Dominican Republic. The teacher made a deal: Anyone who could recite all of the countries and their capitals would be allowed to leave a little early. Luis made a plan:

"I knew I had a good memory, so I volunteered to go first. Sure enough, I got them all right. I went home early!

"From that point on, I knew that my memory was an asset I could rely on to overcome one of my weaknesses: a tendency to procrastinate and wait until the last minute to prepare for tests. Through high school, I was able to memorize the layout of my textbooks (a form of photographic memory) and easily recall information during tests based on its location on the page. This served me well until college. I attended a small liberal arts school where assignments required more critical thinking. As a result, it took me a while to adjust to the new demands of college. What had helped me succeed earlier in life had also kept me from developing the other skills I needed to be successful in higher education."

Pause and Reflect

Take a moment to consider the *game of school:*

- Did you play the game of school? Did you know you were playing?
- What might have happened if you had struggled with one or two of the "rules?"
- Is there a connection between how you played the game of school, and your assumptions and beliefs about learners and learning?
- Do you see the influence of the game of school in your school or classroom?
- Are there parts of the game you don't think will change? Why?

The Game Changer

Our learners may be able to play the game of school up to a certain point, but as they progress through school and the demands increase, this becomes more challenging.

UDL changes the rules of the game. It recognizes that for some learners the game of school is difficult, if not impossible, to play. Rather than one pathway around the board and strict rules, UDL encourages multiple pathways and includes flexible rules to broaden, rather than narrow, who can play. With this in mind, go to the "Next Steps" section (page 42) to apply what you learned, or continue reading if you are ready to go deeper into how the system reinforces our assumptions and beliefs.

Shallow Swim: System Assumptions and Beliefs

Many of us naturally and regularly examine our assumptions and beliefs. We seek to not only confirm and validate what we see and do in our classroom, but also actively seek out research and opinions that challenge our norms. Although this is important to do as a professional, we still have to navigate within the current system.

Beyond the individual assumptions and beliefs you each bring with you from your own experiences in schools are the many assumptions and beliefs about learners and learning that are embedded in the education system—subjects, rows, marks and grades, and testing. Some assumptions and beliefs are so embedded we fail to see them, let alone examine them. There are multiple gorillas in the room.

These long-held, system-level beliefs can make it more difficult when you want to revise or replace some of your own assumptions. When you do challenge them, you often can only go so far before the system blocks additional change. You may encounter vocal opponents who are happy with the status quo. For example, educators who have taught in a particular way for years may have no intention of changing their practice. Parents who are used to the system could be resistant to change, concerned about their children's ability to get into their colleges of choice. Students who excel in the current system might object. Even the administration, fearful of pushback from staff, parents, students, or their own superiors, might be hesitant to tackle big issues. In addition, the requirements of the system—standards, curriculum coverage, grades, report cards, college requirements, grants, funding, and so on—make it difficult to veer very far off the current course.

Assumptions and beliefs, beyond being deeply ingrained, are also complex and interconnected. Sometimes they are simply the result of TTWWADI: That's the way we've always done it. For instance, years ago at an educational technology conference, Kendra heard the story of a small school with two entrances, only one of which was ever used. One teacher began to question why and eventually discovered that, many years before, the school started using the one set of doors while the second set was being repaired. The repairs took from the end of one school year, over summer break, and into the next year, so using the single set of doors became the norm over time. It was just the way things were done, and no one had previously stopped to consider why.

Now, you may say, doors are one thing, but ideas, such as assessment and tests, are another. We don't rely on one type of assessment because of TTWWADI—do we?

Testing 1, 2, 3

Let's put tests to the TTWWADI test by considering the assumptions and beliefs surrounding current testing practices. Rather than standardized tests, which we currently have little authority to reduce or change, think about teacher-designed tests and quizzes. Administered at the end of the week or a unit of study, these tests are generally paper-and-pencil tasks created to evaluate students' content and procedural knowledge. They include all the math, spelling, history, science, and reading tests that require a student to read the instructions and then write their answers or circle the correct response. The design and delivery of these types of tests are based on the assumptions and beliefs associated with four areas: ability, motivation, learning, and assessment. The following outlines the underlying assumptions and beliefs often associated with tests:

Ability

- Students are able to read the test and write the answers.
- Students are able to understand the cultural references embedded in the test.
- Students have English language proficiency.
- Students are able to focus and persist in the completion of the test.
- Bell curves are a natural occurrence; some students will do well, others will fail.
- Results without technology support are superior to results with technology support.

Motivation

- Students will pass the test if they study.
- A low score on a test will motivate students to try harder.
- Tests and the accompanying grade motivate students; they wouldn't bother to learn if we didn't test them.

Learning

- Tests are a good way for students to demonstrate their learning.
- Learning is measured by how well students remember facts, information, algorithms, and so on, and this measurement of understanding is best captured by a test.
- Tests (and the accompanying grade or percentage) provide students with feedback about their learning.
- Tests accurately reflect student's understanding of the material or concepts.

Assessment—Validity/Reliability

- Tests are the most valid and reliable means of measuring student learning.
- Summative assessment supports student learning.
- Grades and percentages are reliable and objective; teacher observation and comments are subjective.
- Tests are important to determine students' marks on their report cards.

Pause and Reflect

Take a moment to quickly respond *yes* or *no* to each of the statements in the list of test assumptions and beliefs. Then:

- Choose one assumption you agree with, then ask yourself: Why do you agree?
- Where did the assumption come from, and how is it confirmed for you?
- Is there any evidence that counters your assumption?
- Repeat these steps with an assumption you disagree with.
- Consider revisiting your assumptions after you explore Chapter 5.

- Tests are the simplest, quickest way to assess students given the size of classes and the demands on teacher time.

What Are We Assessing?

Usually, when a test is created, little attention is given to the reading and writing requirements and their impact on the final outcome. If students fail a history, math, or science test, the reasoning is they didn't study, know the material, or care. The common belief is that students who score poorly on the test need to put in more effort, to try harder.

One reason for these beliefs is that written tests are based on the assumption that everyone should be able to read the text. If a student can't, that student, rather than the test, has a deficit or disability. To access technology or other accommodations to support completion of the test, students often require a label identifying the disability and a legal document in the form of an individual education plan or program (IEP). Even with this in place, students often need to actively seek out and request the extra support or accommodations. This need for a label or special request emphasizes the belief that the accommodation seeker is "different." The assumption is that success requires a certain standard, and the standard must be met independently (for example, without technology). Dr. Dave Edyburn coined the phrase *naked independence* to label the belief that brain power alone is superior to any "assisted" mental activities (Edyburn, 2006). As such, when students are provided technology accommodations, these tools are available only if they are not viewed as providing an unfair advantage. In many cases, even if technology support is provided during regular class time, students must shut off the support features during a test. The assumption is, students need to show their work on their own without the advantage of technology (Figure 4.3). Imagine if we applied this to another support technology, such as students' prescription glasses?

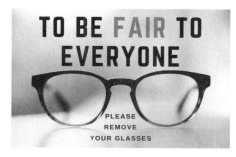

Figure 4.3 Do you think someone who wears glasses in class is cheating?

> **Tweet:** We don't tell students who wear glasses that they are cheating because they see better with the help of lenses. How is using technology to learn better any different? #DiveIntoUDL

With this in mind, go to the "Next Steps" section (page 42) to apply what you've learned, or you can continue to the next section if you are ready to take a deep dive into leading change and challenging embedded, systemic assumptions and beliefs.

Deep Dive: Leading the Change

It is important to recognize that your individual assumptions and beliefs about teaching and learning are influenced by your personal experiences, as well as by the assumptions and beliefs embedded in the education system. Although you may enthusiastically dive into change, regularly challenging your assumptions and beliefs to transform your classroom, you may find others resist this sort of disequilibrium. Whether you are called upon to champion large-scale change within your school or district, or, whether on a smaller scale, you want to share and grow professionally with colleagues, you may encounter assumptions and beliefs that are deeply held, slowing down and even halting the change you know your school and learners need.

Assumptions and beliefs are deeply ingrained. They filter how we perceive the world, influence what we see (or don't see), and determine how we will act. As educators, our professional reputations are based on our skills as pedagogical experts, and these skills are on display every day in the classroom. Examining our assumptions and beliefs, admitting their flaws, and committing to change, are very private and, at the same time, very public activities. As such, many educators hold firmly to their beliefs and resist altering what they do, because it is viewed as integral to who they are (Owston, 2004). But unless we actively challenge our assumptions and beliefs, most change is temporary. As Stephanie Hirsh and Joellen Killion wrote, "When practices change without deep exploration of the principles that guide them, people will be pulled back to their old ways" (2007, p. 21).

Struggling to change isn't just an individual problem, but a system one as well. The call for system change, to transform education, is constant. Most agree it is necessary, yet it seems little changes. Like individuals, districts function on assumptions and beliefs. If these are not explored, challenged, and updated, each initiative becomes just another in a long line of initiatives—all enthusiastically rolled out then quietly forgotten. In "The Power of Beliefs and Assumptions" chapter of its *Becoming a Learning System* course book, Learning Forward made this clear, "Many educational change initiatives fail because leaders focus too much on actions and not enough on their underlying assumptions. New behaviors often are not sustained over time because people's beliefs have not been transformed, and the principles and assumptions needed to sustain the effort are not deeply embedded in the individuals and organization" (2014, p. 13).

When you're trying to lead it, this type of change is challenging and messy work. You want to be action-oriented, so you focus on a plan. You outline the steps, assign people to be responsible, create a timeline, and determine metrics to calculate success. All this busyness can ignore the assumptions and beliefs that should underpin, but are in opposition to, the plan. You're placing the action cart before its team of horses: the assumptions and

⏸ *Pause and Reflect*

As Margaret Wheatley wrote, "I've found that I can only change how I act if I stay aware of my beliefs and assumptions. Thoughts always reveal themselves in behavior. As humans, we often contradict ourselves—we say one thing and do another. We state who we are, but then act contrary to that. We say we're open-minded, but then judge someone for their appearance. We say we're a team, but then gossip about a colleague" (2010, p. 22).

To help you stay aware of how your beliefs and assumptions reveal themselves and affect your students, take a moment to complete the chart in Figure 4.4. You can add your own assumptions, as well, to personalize it. Consider using it with other educators formally or informally to begin the messy work of examining assumptions and beliefs. You might also want to create a similar chart for your district.

Assumption/Belief (What I say)	Action (What do I do)	Reality (What others experience)
Treat all students fairly		
Give students ownership of their learning		
Include summative assessment practice		
Create a safe, welcoming classroom		

Figure 4.4 Chart your assumptions, actions, and impact to help begin sustainable change.

beliefs. Transforming individual assumptions and beliefs and embedding them in the system must come first. Being a leader requires you to advocate for change, share the vision for the change, and then model the process for change you want to see. It requires you to be vulnerable, to be willing to talk about difficult topics and have your assumptions and beliefs challenged.

In all this discussion about assumptions and beliefs, one thing is often missing: students. They are integral to the education system, and they too have assumptions and beliefs about themselves, the purpose of schools, and the way things work. They are more perceptive than we think. Even if they don't express it, they often notice when our assumptions and beliefs do not align with our actions in the classroom. For example, we hear such terms as *student agency*, *student ownership of learning*, *voice and choice*, and *student-centered instruction*, yet, when students enter the classroom, all the traditional accoutrements are there: rows, bells, tests, text-based instruction.

It isn't enough to say we want these things for students. We have to examine our assumptions and beliefs about student ownership and leadership. It requires shared ownership and balance.

The Educator as Collaborator and Facilitator

Most of you have probably heard the advice that educators should move from being the "sage on the stage" to being a "guide on the side" (King, 1993, p. 30). The ISTE Standards for Educators ask you to move beyond both these roles, urging you to get into the thick of it and learn with your students. This is clearly defined within the role of Collaborator (ISTE, 2017), which encourages educators "to redefine their relationship with their students as they model collaboration and facilitate authentic co-learning experiences" (Indicator 4b).

Currently, educators are considered pedagogical experts. In many ways, this assumption and belief is true; educators have studied and trained to become skilled at their craft. The traditional view assumes the educator, as the expert, is responsible for determining the goals, methods, materials, and assessments to be used in the lesson. Educators are also often considered subject specialists as well, especially in the higher grades. Again as experts, they have the jobs of determining what content is important to know and delivering it to their students. With the advent of mobile technology and the means to easily create and share content, however, students are no longer dependent on the teacher for their content—or learning. Outside of the classroom they can pursue any topic that interests them, in virtually any format. These seismic shifts have heightened the need to shift the role of the teacher. Although pedagogical expertise is still important, the hierarchy of the classroom is quickly being replaced with environments where the teacher is a co-learner, modeling learning as a collaborative, connected, and shared experience.

The ISTE Standards for Educators (2017) signal not only a change in what teachers do, but also a shift in control. For many educators, their role is clearly defined, established by decades of tradition. Ownership and control of learning is based on the assumption that teachers lead and students follow. It is the educator's job to create the lesson, then teach it and test how well students understood it. It is the student's job to learn the material, complete assignments, and take the assessments. Even educators who embrace changes to their role often struggle with the release of responsibility for learning to students. They also struggle against system assumptions and beliefs that reinforce the status quo. Report cards, standard parent-teacher conferences, curriculum maps, and standardized tests place decision-making and ownership of learning in the hands of the teacher.

The Educator Standards also highlight significant shifts in ownership through the role of Facilitator (ISTE, 2017), in which educators are encouraged to "foster a culture where students take ownership of their learning goals and outcomes in both independent and group settings" (Indicator 6a). To "foster a culture of ownership" the educator is encouraged to profoundly change the student-teacher dynamic by guiding students to assume an active role in the why and how of their learning. In essence, students are to shape and maintain the learning and social culture of the classroom, but they may not always be ready to take on this role as co-designers of learning right away. You can help your students develop classroom leadership skills by showing that you trust them and their abilities to grow into a shared role. You can do this by:

- Providing students with opportunities to set and pursue personal goals that extend beyond a single lesson or unit to the entire school year. These goals may be related to personal qualities, specific skills, or passions students want to pursue. To benefit the rest of the class, students would be asked to provide regular status reports during which they share what they are learning and ask for support from peers who have a similar interest.

- Actively involving students in the development of classroom norms that are revisited and revised as classroom events warrant throughout the year.

These steps show students that you follow through on your stated beliefs when it comes to their ownership of learning. You don't just pay lip service to them, but actually put your evolving assumptions about learning into practice as you redefine classroom roles. Shifting the responsibility for learning to your students will help them develop their self-regulation, metacognition, and self-efficacy, some of the qualities that define an expert learner under UDL.

Next Steps

Our assumptions and beliefs are complex. They are a combination of what we've learned, and what we've experienced. They can, just like our clothes, be outdated, worn, and difficult to throw away. Our assumptions and beliefs about learners and learning, however, ultimately determine what our classrooms look and sound like. Too often, if we don't critically examine our assumptions and beliefs, what we *say* we believe and what we *do* in the classroom are in direct opposition. Although it can be uncomfortable to critically examine our long-held assumptions, it is crucial to continually revise and update them. We must also be open to having our assumptions and beliefs challenged, not just by colleagues with whom we

❚❚ *Pause and Reflect*

If you lead an upcoming workshop or presentation to staff/faculty, consider how you can model the shift to co-learning. You may decide to ask participants to set the goals and agenda for the session; include virtual participants/guests; and provide options for what people learn and a variety of resources and materials to model accessibility.

Brainstorm (perhaps in a Google Doc) all the objections that might come up when discussing profound changes to roles, learning, and classroom culture. Then list proactive ways to acknowledge, overcome, or go around the problems. You might also include links to videos or blogs that dive deeper into the question. This document will help you refine your thinking, and act as a resource as you work with other educators. Consider sharing this document so others can add their own thoughts or links, or create a new document with a team of educators as an ongoing exploration of the changes that are required to keep moving forward. Together you could also create a "Now/Future" T-chart to compare and contrast the traditional classroom culture to one in which ownership and learning is shared. Consider adding a rating scale (1 - Now, 5 - Future) to assess where you are as a staff/school, and then consider ways to move toward the future. As you work through the process, make sure to reference the Facilitator role in the ISTE Standards for Educators.

agree, but also by those who may see things differently. Like individuals, systems also hold assumptions and beliefs. Although we often recognize policies, procedures, and programs are outdated and in need of change, we fail to recognize that the underlying assumptions and beliefs, firmly embedded and interconnected in the daily routines of the system, are also in need of repair and replacement.

The ISTE Standards for Educators (2017) can help frame and guide discussions about assumptions and beliefs at both the individual and system level. As a leader, you need the courage and conviction to be willing to relinquish some control as you transfer some of the responsibility for learning to students. As a Collaborator and Facilitator for learning *with* your students, you will show them that they have your trust as partners in the nurturing of a classroom culture built around shared values and norms. This transfer of control and responsibility for learning may be one of the most difficult shifts for educators to make, but it may also be the one that results in the most significant transformation of learning from something that happens to students to something they can do for themselves as expert learners.

> **Tweet:** Our assumptions and beliefs about learners and learning ultimately determine what our classrooms look and sound like. If we don't critically examine our assumptions and beliefs, what we say we believe and what we do in the classroom are in direct opposition. #DiveIntoUDL

Website Activities

To delve even deeper into this subject, scan the QR code to access additional information, videos, and other digital resources related to this chapter on the companion website.

UDL Assumptions and Beliefs

I n Chapter 4, you examined your own assumptions and beliefs, now it's time to explore UDL's. As we mentioned in the introduction, UDL originally focused on removing barriers for those learners "in the margins" (Meyer and Rose, 2005). Over time, its assumptions and beliefs expanded beyond this "medical model," or special education approach, to encompass three broad levels: access, build, and internalize. At their core, UDL's assumptions and beliefs are about providing *equity* for all learners in a proactive, systematic way.

To help visualize UDL's values, goals, and proactive approach, consider Figure 5.1, which is titled "Equality versus Equity." Each panel represents a different approach for ensuring that everyone can enjoyably watch a baseball game.

The left panel in Figure 5.1 represents our current system. With the goal of "fairness," each child is provided with the same means of viewing the game. This situation is analogous to traditional learning environments that are designed around one-size-fits-all solutions. Learners are provided with the same type of instruction, materials, and methodologies, and they are assessed in the same way, regardless of their starting point. Is this really fair? As Richard

Figure 5.1 Equality versus equity: If the goal is for everyone to watch the game, then the means should match the needs, and preferences, of the viewer.

Lavoie, best known for his video "How Difficult Can This Be?" said, "Our definition of fair in education is at the 5th grade level. Fair doesn't mean everyone gets the same. It means everyone gets what they need" (1989).

In the right panel, everyone can see the game. Their variability in height and preference was taken into consideration and a variety of levels of support were offered. This arrangement is more equitable and fair in the sense that each child has access to a variety of tools and methods they can use to successfully look over the fence. In many ways, this represents the accommodations model we currently use in education. Each learner is provided with supports and aids based on individual need after those needs are identified. This reactive approach to the variability of learners assumes the learner is the problem, however.

Although the right panel is an improvement over the left in terms of the level of equity, its solution is limited by its assumption that the fence is necessary (or at the very least, immovable). If watching the game is the goal, then looking over the fence *unaided* is the benchmark. Although the supports are distributed equitably based on need in the right panel, the assumption is the baseball fan that can look over the fence without support, without the technology of a box, is superior to the one who needs multiple supports. It approaches the person as having a deficit. The fence isn't seen as the problem, the person is. This happens in classrooms everyday, where we assume our goals, methods, materials, and assessments are designed fairly. They are not viewed as having any flaws. Because everyone gets the same, the belief is that no one receives an unfair advantage. Those who can't keep up, read the materials, write the report, or complete the test are considered less capable than their peers, as if the problem is with them rather than the design of the goals, methods, materials, or assessment.

Figure 5.2 Changing assumptions leads to better solutions: from equal to equity to removing systemic barriers.

Now consider Figure 5.2. The new rightmost panel represents a more proactive approach. It recognizes where the disability lay: the board fence. The barrier in the environment that kept all three bystanders from being able to enjoy the baseball game has been removed altogether. As such, regardless of the height of any new people who show up, there will not be any need to provide a support. Considering variability ahead of time made the support unnecessary. This approach to variability, based on providing equity for all learners in a proactive and systematic way, is what UDL is all about. With UDL, we can and do assess learners, but we do so in such a way that does not creates barriers. Back to our classroom example, instead of requiring every learner to complete only text-based activities, which puts students who struggle with reading and writing at a disadvantage, we could provide a menu of options for learners to access information and demonstrate their understanding. This removes the barrier associated with print (the board fence) from the goal of the assessment (watching the baseball game).

Pause and Reflect

Think about your classroom. Are there any fences that create unnecessary barriers for your students? Create a list, and then, with your students' help, look for ways to remove the barriers.

Can you think of another image that would represent the difference between equality and equity? Are there any other assumptions and beliefs represented in the "Equality versus Equity" image that you would alter? If you added a fourth panel, what else could change? Consider creating your own image as a quick sketch using an app, such as Procreate (Savage Interactive), or with an online tool, such as Canva (**canva.com**), and share your ideas with us on social media using the hashtag #DiveIntoUDL. You can find our fourth panel image on the book's companion website (**DiveIntoUDL.com**).

Key Assumptions

In this chapter, you will explore six key assumptions of UDL (Figure 5.3) that form the foundation for the UDL Guidelines, which Chapter 6 examines in detail.

To help you put theory into practice quickly and easily, we have organized this chapter based on levels of abstraction, as well as changes that happen at the instructional level. At a high level, the "Wade In" section focuses on access to information and learning, the "Shallow Swim" section on student ownership of assessment and learning, and the "Deep Dive" section on developing learner expertise:

- **Wade In: Creating an "All-Access" Classroom for Learning** (page 49). In this section, you will explore the assumptions and beliefs UDL makes about disability and accessibility. These are often at odds with our current system, which focuses on identifying disability and providing support technology to only those who are "disabled." You'll then focus on how to reduce barriers and support accessibility in your instructional design. You can start implementing the insights gained from this section in your very next lesson.

- **Shallow Swim: Build Skills for Ownership of Learning** (page 59). In this section, you will examine UDL's assumptions and beliefs about equitable assessment and ownership of

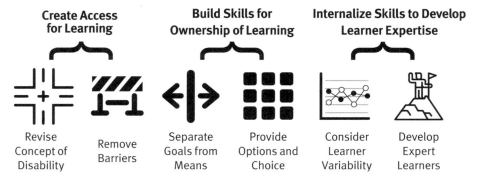

Figure 5.3 UDL's assumptions and beliefs are layered and interconnected. *Expert Learner icon by monkik from flaticon.com*

learning. These are often in opposition to our current system, which emphasizes easily measured text-based assessment used for evaluation purposes, rather than for feedback, or student self-reflection and metacognition. You will then go on to explore how to create more flexible lessons with options and choice for learners, giving them ownership over how they access, process, produce, and share their learning.

- **Deep Dive: Internalize Skills to Develop Learner Expertise** (page 65). In this section, you will investigate UDL's assumptions and beliefs about variability and the purpose of school. These are often resisted by the current system, which focuses on the average student, as defined by the content knowledge and academic skills it is believed students need to know at each grade level. This section, which discusses the development of learning expertise, is more abstract and asks you to redesign your instruction by taking into consideration UDL's assumptions and beliefs from the outset.

Once again, you have the opportunity to choose your level. This could be based on your self-assessment from Chapter 3 or your interest after reading the summaries provided. The choice is yours! We encourage you to revisit this chapter from time to time to reflect on your continuing growth as a UDL practitioner.

> **Tweet:** UDL's Assumptions & Beliefs create accessible and equitable learning environments that promote student ownership & learner expertise. #DiveIntoUDL

Wade In: Creating an All-Access Classroom for Learning

UDL makes two related assumptions that turn traditional thinking about disability and accessibility upside down:

- What we perceive as disability is often a poor fit between learners and their learning environment.
- To create a more inclusive classroom, it is imperative that we remove barriers to information and learning.

Let's examine each assumption more closely, and then discuss ways to address them in your classroom.

Assumption 1: Examine the Fit Between Learners and Environment

For much of the history of education the focus has been primarily on the individual characteristics of learners, while the learning *environment* (whether it is the curriculum or the physical environment of the classroom) has been mostly taken as a given. One way this has happened is with the close association between education and the ability to read print.

We tend to ignore the limitations of print as a fixed format that does not offer the flexibility needed to accommodate variable learners. Thus, when a learner struggles to read or has difficulty with decoding print, we assign that learner a label and say he or she has a disability. With UDL, we don't take the environment as a given. We explore the many ways in which the learning environment can be both disabled and disabling to some learners. From this perspective, *disability is not inherent to the learner, but arises when there is a bad fit between his and her variability and the learning environment.*

A great story that exemplifies the traditional fixation on the "fault" of the learner comes from CAST instructional designer and good friend Mindy Johnson. As a child, Mindy experienced firsthand the effects of a bad fit between learning variability and learning environment when her mother made her (under protest) take piano lessons. Each week the teacher would bring out the sheet music, and Mindy would try to read the notes. The teacher used all kinds of tricks and reminders, but nothing worked. The assumption was that Mindy would never be a great pianist if she couldn't learn to read music.

With the help of her mother, Mindy disproved this assumption. Each night, Mindy's mom played her daughter's homework. Mindy listened, and the next day she easily could play what she had heard the night before. Everyone thought she had learned to read the notes, when in reality she was playing by ear.

When Mindy attended competitions she would win if she was able to prepare and rehearse ahead of time. Whenever the judges put sheet music in front of her, however, she couldn't play it. Depending on the context, Mindy was either gifted, based on her superior listening ability for music, or disabled, based on her inability to interpret and make use of the sheet music in front of her.

> **Tweet:** Learning is contextual. If your students are not learning, consider changing the context and/or environment to better support learning. #DiveIntoUDL

A similar scenario plays out in classrooms all over the world. A learner who struggles in a curriculum that is heavily based on print may blossom when provided with other options for accessing and processing information, such as audio books or digital text that can be customized or read aloud with text to speech. When a plant struggles to grow we don't just focus on the plant itself, we also consider the environmental conditions and whether they can support growth with the right mix of nutrients (Figure 5.4). Similarly, with UDL we don't just focus on the needs of the learner, we also consider the affordances of the environment and the fit between the two. From this perspective, disability is a design challenge; the goal is to create a better fit for the learner by designing a more flexible learning environment that can accommodate variability.

Figure 5.4 Treat your learners like plants. Be willing to find the right conditions and optimal environment for learning and growth.

Pause and Reflect

Do you have learners who are disabled by the methods and means available to them in the classroom? Many learners find success outside the classroom, in sports, the arts, social events, or coding. How could you use these outside strengths to support ability in your classroom?

Universal Design

If a single context is not appropriate for all learners, then how can we design flexibility into the context to ensure it does not place any of our learners at a disadvantage? The approach known as *Universal Design*, which inspired UDL, provides a workable solution. Originating in the field of architecture, Universal Design is a proactive approach to design. Architect Ron Mace, a pioneer of the movement, described Universal Design as "The design of products and environments to be usable by all people, to the greatest extent possible, without the need for adaptation or specialized design" (Center for Universal Design, 2008). A good example of Universal Design can be found in the design of older buildings. Many of these buildings did not originally allow access to individuals in wheelchairs, and so ramps, often unsightly and expensive, were added as retrofits. Frequently, these ramps were placed in areas that were convenient for the architect and the builder, such as at the rear or far side of a building, but not for those who needed them. The "go around to the back" approach to access emphasized the user was different and needed "special" access. In the classroom, an example of a similar retrofit is the use of accommodations to address learner differences.

In places where ramps were conveniently installed, many people found they could use the ramp based on need or choice. Ramp use extended beyond that of individuals in wheelchairs; parents pushing strollers and delivery people pushing equipment on a cart or packages on a dolly were among the most common users. Even better, as Universal Design began to take hold in the world of architecture, many designers began to abandon

Pause and Reflect

Once you become aware of Universal Design, it seems to pop up everywhere (Figure 5.5). Think about the various places you have been or the tools you have used in the past few days. How many examples of Universal Design can you come up with? How did these various examples of Universal Design make the task easier for someone with a "disability?" How did they make the task easier for everyone else?

Figure 5.5 An example of Universal Design, these stairs in Robson Square, Vancouver, BC, were designed (not retrofitted) by architect Arthur Erickson to provide multiple ways to make it to the top.

the idea of ramps altogether, by designing entrances without any stairs at all. This resulted in "front door" access for everyone, as well as more aesthetically pleasing designs. (For more information on the history and growth of Universal Design and its principles, see **universaldesign.ie/ What-is-Universal-Design**.)

Applying Universal Design to Your Classroom

With Universal Design for Learning, you can apply the same "front door" approach to your curriculum. Rather than waiting for individual learners to require retrofits and accommodations that can be costly and time-consuming, you can plan ahead for the variability you know will be present in every classroom. One way to do this is by designing lessons that include a number of options for learners to access the content and express what they have learned. With technology, this might mean providing *all* students—not just those who struggle with written language—with such options as recording their voices on a computer or tablet, or using word-prediction or speech-to-text tools. It might mean giving them options to create a short film or infographic as an alternative to a written report. With these options, not only are you providing diverse learners more options with which to show their understanding, you are providing an outlet for their creativity that can result in better engagement.

This last point is a key difference between Universal Design for Learning and the Universal Design movement in architecture and product design. Because UDL is concerned with learning, it takes into account learners' motivation and emotional disposition for learning, not just the accessibility of the learning environment. Ensuring the environment is flexible from the start and provides access with a minimum of effort is an important step toward ensuring a positive learning experience for all—but it is just a first step. If too many barriers exist and learners have to spend a lot of effort to overcome them, this can impact their desire to learn and some may not persist with the learning task.

> **Tweet:** UDL is the application of #UD to learning. It takes into account learners' motivation and emotional disposition for learning, not just the accessibility of the learning environment. #DiveIntoUDL

To put the link between accessibility and motivation into perspective, consider visiting a website with poor design. Although you want the information it contains, you spend considerable time simply trying to determine how the site works because neither the interface nor navigation are intuitive and the text, images, and structure are poorly designed. You give up in frustration before you even address the content. The website's designer neglected the user experience (UX). When designing instruction we educators must not neglect the *learner experience* (LX). As Dorian

> ## ❚❚ *Pause and Reflect*
>
> Consider a recent lesson you implemented. What aspects of the design related to reading, writing, focus, and organization may have interfered with the learning? What could you do differently to remove the barriers you found?

Peters, a specialist in design for learning and well-being, asked in a *UX Magazine* article, "Did [my students] learn something in spite of the way this was designed, or because of it?" (Peters, 2011).

Assumption 2: Remove Barriers to Information and Learning

UDL is based on the belief that *we must proactively and intentionally remove barriers to the access to information and, more importantly, to learning.* In fact, until recently removing barriers was often the focus of most discussions about UDL. Although there's much more to UDL than this, removing barriers is still a very important first step. More importantly, it is an excellent way to immediately apply UDL principles to your practice. Without it, learners are still divided in their access to information by ability. Their potential and ability to demonstrate their learning are restricted by this lack of access. By considering the barriers in your resources, methods, and tools and by adding technology support, you can remove "fences" to create a more equitable, all-access classroom.

Digital, but Still Inaccessible

Frequently in discussions of removing barriers, digital access and tools are the "low-hanging fruits" picked as a solution. Simply providing learning materials in a digital format does not automatically make a lesson accessible to learners. As CAST instructional designer Mindy Johnson stated, "Born digital doesn't mean born accessible." Every format has limitations

Pause and Reflect

Watch "Joe's Non-Netbook" at **bit.ly/DiveIntoUDLCh5a**, or take a look at Figure 5.6.

- In what ways is the printed page inaccessible?
- What types of access and support did the students want?
- What other features of digital text could support the learners in your class?

Figure 5.6 "Joe's Non-Netbook" questions the accessibility of print books.

and barriers. If we assume that digital is automatically accessible, we may be ignoring, or even creating other barriers to learning for our students. That is why with UDL we provide multiple means and do not rely on one format—even digital.

Consider the example of a teacher who scans the print version of a worksheet into a PDF document. Although digital, is the file text-based or image-based? In other words, was the document scanned as an image file, in essence locking the text inside a picture, or was it scanned using optical character recognition (OCR), so the words in the document are saved as readable text? If the PDF is an image-based PDF, the text will be inaccessible to the text-to-speech technology many learners need to support their reading.

> **Tweet:** No single format is 100% accessible. Provide choice, and learners will be more likely to find the format that works best for a given task. #DiveIntoUDL

Even when text is accessible in a digital format, you need to consider if the *learning* is accessible. Are there physical, cultural, language, or experience barriers that also need to be addressed? Do students need additional supports to address the barriers to the learning embedded in the digital resource?

Read the following passage. Most likely only one or two words are unfamiliar to you. As you read, imagine that you struggle with printed text and the passage is being read out loud by a screen reader. Would this help your comprehension?

The evaporation rate from porous media often exhibits an abrupt transition from a high and nearly constant rate supplied by capillary-induced liquid flow (stage 1) to lower values supported by vapor diffusion. Evidence suggests that evaporation from hydrophobic porous media is suppressed relative to evaporation from similar hydrophilic media. The mechanism for evaporation suppression remains unclear; some implicate effects of partial wettability on liquid phase continuity. Here we examine potential effects of wettability on capillary driving forces required for sustaining liquid flows. Evaporation experiments from sand-filled columns with different fractions of hydrophobic grains enabled comparisons of evaporative mass loss rates and drying front depths. Results show a gradual reduction in drying front depth at the end of stage 1 (denoted as "evaporation characteristic length") with an increasing fraction of hydrophobic grains.

Citation: Shokri, N., P. Lehmann, and D. Or (2009), Characteristics of evaporation from partially wettable porous media, *Water Resour. Res.*, 45, W02415, doi:10.1029/2008WR007185.

If the example passage were available only in a textbook or as a note on the board, it would be inaccessible to many students. The first barrier would be access to information (content). However, the second barrier would be access to learning (context). Even if you provided the passage in a digital format with, perhaps, the option to have the text read out loud, that would address only access to information. Access to learning would still be blocked. To address this barrier, you might include vocabulary support, a video of background information, guiding questions, or a graphic organizer to support and guide comprehension. If the text was in a digital format, these supports could be built into the passage, making the options for support seamless and available to all.

Pause and Reflect

What might a "barrier-free" classroom look and sound like? Beyond first-level barriers, those imposed by the nature of their design, also consider second-level barriers, those imposed by our assumptions and beliefs as well as the limitations of our current technology. One method is to create a T-chart, and then think back to a recent classroom activity. List all the barriers on the left side, and on the right side, list the tools, methods, and materials you could use to remove the barrier. As you complete the list, consider the assumptions and beliefs that guide your choices. Alternately, do this activity with your students, having them highlight and find ways to remove barriers with you.

You can now go to the "Next Steps" section (page 75) to apply what you've learned or continue to the next section to investigate more of UDL's assumptions.

Shallow Swim: Build Skills for Ownership of Learning

UDL makes two assumptions related to the gradual release of responsibility for learning to learners, and how this impacts the traditional roles of student and teacher:

- Separating the goals of learning from the means of demonstrating competency can bring greater equity and agency to assessment.
- Learners need options and choice to address their learning needs, strengths, and preferences and to prepare them to drive their own learning.

In this section, we will explore each assumption more closely and then discuss how these fundamental shifts impact everything from goal setting to curriculum decisions to assessment practices.

Assumption 3: Separate Content Goals from Skill Goals

Often, barriers to learning exist not in the physical environment or the tools and materials we choose for our lessons, but in the way we frame instructional goals and expectations. Another key assumption of UDL is that *knowledge goals, related to the understanding of concepts, ideas, and facts should, when possible, be separate from skill goals, such as writing an essay, giving a speech, or computation.* Often goals are confounded. What we think is a single goal is actually two. This occurs when the means of attaining the goal are linked with the goal itself. This disconnect is based on the assumption that every student lacks the knowledge we have (and we need to teach them), but already possesses the skills needed to demonstrate the knowledge. This is particularly true in middle and high school where the focus shifts to separate subjects. Students read from textbooks and write reports, essays, and tests with little consideration as to whether these methods and materials block some learners from the information they need or the ability to express what they learned.

For example, consider two typical learning goals: "The student will express their understanding of the causes of the Civil War in a three-minute speech" and "The student will write a five-paragraph essay on the importance of the building of a national railway to the nation's development."

Both statements actually represent two goals each:

- A skill goal, such as writing an essay or delivering a speech
- A concept goal that includes historical understanding

With UDL, we seek to separate these goals, or in other words, to separate the goal from the means for achieving it. Suppose the goal is understanding the importance of a historical event. Learners can demonstrate this knowledge in a way that acknowledges their varying strengths and needs: They could share their insights about the event by recording an audio reflection or a video, for example, or they could even re-enact the event in class using a variety of props. When we limit learners to just writing their responses or presenting in class, learners who struggle with that mode of expression can be put at a disadvantage that can blur or obscure their true level of understanding.

UDL researcher Todd Rose expressed the core problem with confounded goals:

> "...it means your weakness will make it hard for us to see, let alone nurture, your talent. We all know kids like this ... The kid who is gifted in science but who's a below average reader. Because our science textbooks assume that every kid is reading at grade level this kid's in trouble, because for her science class is first and foremost a reading test, and it's doubtful that we will ever see what she's truly capable of." (TEDx Talks, 2013)

Separate Goals and Means

A good place to start with the idea of separating goals from the means of achievement is to determine early in the planning process whether your goal is a knowledge or skill goal, as this will determine the kind of flexibility you can provide your learners. A *knowledge goal* expresses what learners should *know* at the end of the lesson or activity, while a *skill goal* focuses on what learners should be able to *do* at the end of the lesson or activity. If, after considering the goal, you determine that it is primarily a knowledge goal, then you can think about providing a variety of options for how learners can show their understanding: writing an essay, recording a podcast, creating an infographic, and so on. If, on the other hand, you determine that the goal primarily focuses on a skill, you can then think about ensuring students understand the processes and procedures associated with the skill and have opportunities to practice and improve. In a UDL version of the example goal regarding the role of the railroad in the nation's history, for instance, learners could be given some choice in the perspective they take on the topic: They could explore the topic from the perspective of the immigrant workers, the railroad owners, the government, and so on. A variety of information resources could be provided, including an interactive timeline, audio resources, videos, books, and websites to give students choice in how they access information on the topic. In addition, you could also provide choice in the tools students use and the product they will create to meet the goal.

Your state or district standards will often impose some constraints in how much flexibility you can exercise in your planning. However, even when a standard is narrowly expressed, you can still provide some flexibility for your learners through appropriate scaffolding. If a standard explicitly requires learners to write a report or essay on a given topic, you could provide a variety of options. For younger learners or English Language Learners, you might provide pictures to help them first retell their story before writing, a graphic organizer to plan each step, or sentence starters to get them on their way. As students mature, you could provide them with access to a concept mapping tool to plan and organize their work, give them opportunities to draw before they write, or suggest they record their thoughts with audio or video prior to sitting down to the task. Of course, technology support by way of text to speech and word prediction (which is standard on many of today's devices) should always be available to everyone. These tools reduce the barriers the goal created, allowing the learner to show higher-level thinking, mastery of the concepts, and the ability to create a logical, evidence-based argument: the important aspects of the goal.

Like adjusting then removing the training wheels on a bike, you would, over time, fade some of these supports as the learners gain skill and become more capable writers. In this way, you would account for their areas of need while still allowing their understanding to come through in the assessment. Remember, however, that for some students, print may be a lifelong barrier. As such, access to technology support should not be viewed as a crutch, discarded when they are healed, but more like glasses, a lifelong necessary tool.

Aside from creating a less equitable environment for some learners, confounding the goals with the means for achieving them also impacts the accuracy of our assessments. When you confound goals, it is difficult to determine if learners were unsuccessful because of a lack of understanding or because they had difficulty with the means of expressing what they know. By more clearly stating the goal, you can ensure that your assessments are construct relevant: They actually measure what they say they measure.

Tweet: Barriers to learning can be embedded in the goals of a lesson. Separate the goals from the means of achieving them to develop construct-relevant assessments that more accurately show your learners' true understanding. #DiveIntoUDL

Pause and Reflect

Have you ever experienced an activity where the means prevented you from demonstrating your skill or understanding? As a result, how did you feel after completing that activity? How would you now redesign that activity to provide alternative means for showing understanding?

Assumption 4: Learners Need Options and Choice

With a clear goal, separated from the means, you have already started to *provide your learners options and choice in how they access information, engage with tasks, process the learning, and then demonstrate their understanding.* Providing options and choice around a reading and writing task is a good place to start, but ultimately all subject areas need to be addressed. Remember, relying on one tool, one resource, one method, or one means is ineffective for learning, assessment, and engagement.

When first creating a UDL environment in your classroom, providing students a choice in the tools and methods they use is an important first step. For instance, you could create a tic-tac-toe board with a variety of app options that learners could use to complete an assignment (Figure 5.7). This method gives you a manageable number of resources and tools to collect and evaluate, and it gives students a manageable number of options from which to choose. For older students, choices could be represented by a posted list or a shared Google Doc where they could post suggestions and reviews. Once students are familiar with the tools and options, and they better understand themselves as learners, you can gradually release the responsibility of choice to the student completely.

Figure 5.7 A tic-tac-toe options board is one way we can add choice into our lessons.

To build even more choice and ownership into your assignments, you could also provide the option for a wild card: Learners could submit their own assignment after getting a list of criteria they have to meet to ensure the submission still fulfills the goals of the lesson or activity. This is a great way to engage learners as co-designers of the lesson or activity, especially for those learners who already have prior knowledge of the topic.

We took the approach of learners as co-designers in an online course on UDL. At the conclusion of each week, our learners (who were educators like yourself) could choose from a variety of assignments at different levels of complexity, but they could also contact us to propose an assignment of their own. As long as the proposed assignment met the focus for the week and moved the participant's learning forward, we were fine with this arrangement. This allowed some learners to apply what they were learning in our course to a specific, personal classroom inquiry question they had, and, in the case of one group, to a district need for change. This approach both highlighted the flexibility UDL entails and helped make the assignment more relevant and meaningful for learners.

When the UDL Guidelines first came out in 2008, it was more challenging to provide students with technology options that allowed them to access, process, produce, and share their learning. Today there are a plethora of mobile devices, tablets, apps, and online resources. As such, it is important to explore, build, and cull your technology toolkit periodically. When choosing tools or resources ask the following question: Who might not be able to use this app, tool, or resource and why? Then, provide alternatives or find a more inclusive app. In addition, most devices today have built-in accessibility features. Exploring these options, using them yourself and sharing with your students truly puts options and choice into the hands of the learner.

> **Tweet:** When choosing tools or resources for your #UDL classroom, ask: Who might not be able to use this app, tool, or resource and why? Then provide alternatives. #DiveIntoUDL

As you explore UDL deeper, choice for learners expands beyond options to choose what tools they will use or the method that best allows them to demonstrate their learning. More profound choice lies in agency and ownership, where students set personally relevant goals, as well as determine what they will learn and how it will be assessed. However, giving learners the option to independently drive their own learning too soon, without proper scaffolds and strategies in place, could result in disaster. Don't worry. We will not let this happen. In Part 3 we will model how to plan and design lessons that support students and pace the gradual release of responsibility for learning to them.

Pause and Reflect

What kinds of options and choice do you provide your students? If they make simple decisions (either/or, pick from a list), how might you expand their choices? How would you prepare them? What scaffolds, strategies, and apps could you use to support students as they gain independence?

You can now go to the "Next Steps" section (page 75) to apply what you've learned or continue to the next section to investigate more of UDL's assumptions.

Deep Dive: Internalize Skills to Develop Learner Expertise

UDL makes two assumptions about the learning environments that are required if we want learners to be self-directed, self-reflective, and self-regulated:

- All learners vary in systematic and predictable ways, and we can account for this variability by developing more flexible learning environments.
- The goal of education is to develop learner expertise. Expert learners are purposeful, motivated, resourceful, knowledge-able, strategic, and goal-directed.

In this section, we will explore each assumption more closely and then discuss how the creation of flexible learning environments is key to addressing the variability of students so that every learner can be an expert learner.

Assumption 5: Address Learner Variability Through Flexible Design

Another key assumption of UDL is that *all learners vary in predictable ways.* In any learning environment, you are always going to get a range of learners with different background knowledge, ways of accessing and processing information, temperaments, and school and home experiences. We teach and assess learners, however, as if there was one "average" learner. As Todd Rose has stated in his presentation "The Myth of Average," when you "design for this mythical average, you actually design for no one" (Tedx Talks, 2013).

Cars are an excellent example of designing for variability rather than the "average." In Henry Ford's era hundreds of thousands of nearly identical cars were mass-produced for the "average" person. Today, cars are designed with a personalized driving experience in mind. You don't have to conform to the car; it is designed to meet your particular needs and preferences. You can adjust the seat and mirrors to address your physical requirements. You can alter conditions, such as temperature, humidity, and even sound, to create an optimal driving environment that leaves you feeling relaxed but alert. In addition, technology continues to improve everything from safety to enjoyment. For example, many cars have a built-in GPS to effectively guide you to your destination without the need for cumbersome paper maps. Perhaps most importantly, you are in control of the car and can make use of the tools and features as needed. If the conditions change, you can slow down or speed up, re-adjust the seat for comfort, and use built-in tools, such as turning on the wipers to give you a clear view.

> ***Tweet:*** As @ltoddrose states, when you design for the average, you design for no one. Give your learners a flexible seat and allow them to customize the learning environment to match their preferences and needs. #DiveIntoUDL

Pause and Reflect

- Where are some areas in your classroom or instruction that you teach to the "average?"
- How did you determine this average?
- In which one area could you address variability in your instruction tomorrow?
- What do you think education would look like if we took the bold step of banning the average?
- What do you think would be the first change you would see?

The need to design for variability seems obvious when we think of cars, yet for the most part, it is ignored in education. The idea of providing options is often voiced but has not, as yet, become fully embedded in the system. We are still stuck with the assembly line approach to education where standardization rules. It brings to mind a quote by Henry Ford, who mastered the assembly line process, mass producing identical (but affordable) cars: "Any customer can have a car painted any color that he wants so long as it is black" (Ford & Crowther, 1922, p. 72).

Ford stubbornly insisted on maintaining the basic design of the Model T, even after other automobile makers began to design cars that appealed to the needs and preferences of the consumer. This disruption, choice, caused his car sales to plummet. Almost too late, Ford recognized that uniformity no longer worked in the automotive industry. Education has also had its share of disruption, often driven by technology and science (Figure 5.8). Whether we heed the evidence that change is required remains to be seen.

FLEXIBLE DESIGN

Puts your students in the driver's seat of their learning.

Figure 5.8 Like drivers on the highway, although all learners are headed toward the same destination, their drive (and route) is personalized.

The field of neuroscience provides compelling evidence that change is needed; many in the field have called into question the idea that an "average brain" exists. Dr. John Medina, a developmental molecular biologist focused on the genes involved in human brain development and the author of Brain Rules (**brainrules.net**), likens our brains to roads: The big freeways are the same in all of us. We all have a hippocampus, for example. The differences happen on the smaller routes: the streets and back roads. Our brains are full of these smaller routes that are shaped by our experiences. As Dr. Medina explained: "If I've heard of Jennifer Aniston and you haven't, I have a Jennifer Aniston neuron and you don't. That's why identical twins don't have identical brains." Until recently brain studies compiled brain scans into one "average" image. As Dr. Aaron Nitzkin, noted in his blog titled, "The Myth of the Average Brain" (2016): Using one amalgamated brain scan to make assumptions about individuals is similar to using one "average" map to find your way around different cities. There may be some similarities, but you will probably get lost. The idea that every student's "brain map" is different is now well accepted and continues to be confirmed by research in neuroscience, if not entirely in our classroom practices.

> **Tweet:** "Our school system ignores the fact that every brain is wired differently. We wrongly assume every brain is the same." Dr. John Medina #DiveIntoUDL

To account for the variability of the learning brain, we educators need to design for flexibility by providing multiple pathways for how learners progress through each learning task. A single pathway or route will not be able to accommodate the varying needs of all individuals. Consider it in terms of our swimming analogy: If the goal is to get to the end of the pool, there are multiple ways for a swimmer (or non-swimmer) to do it. Some swimmers may need a life jacket as they learn to coordinate their limbs (and not sink). Others may use a kickboard or even water wings, to give a bit of support as they make their way across the pool. Some swimmers may swim close to the side of the pool, grabbing the side to take breaks as needed. Some swimmers may be focused on perfecting their strokes and improving their time. And still others might be ready to race back and forth, incorporating a variety of strokes as they challenge themselves to improve. In other words, there are all sorts of ways to swim and get to the same destination—or achieve the same goal in a learning context (Figure 5.9).

Figure 5.9 Is your school an average pool, or does it support variability?

Now consider if the swimming experience was designed like a traditional classroom learning experience: There would be only one way through the water, an average water depth, and an average pool length. For those starting out, this might be too challenging or even dangerous. For those who are average swimmers, there would be little challenge, no way to grow or develop their skills. They might quickly tire of doing the same thing and turn to a different activity that is more fun. For those who are capable of competing in the individual medley, the average route is too easy. They will easily get across the pool with little effort only to sit on the side and wait for the rest to catch up. Having our expert swimmers help others could be dangerous, and it isn't an acceptable alternative to providing the right amount of challenge from the outset.

Pause and Reflect

- Do the learners described in the swimming example describe any of your learners?
- How are you ensuring there is not a single pathway for all learners in your classroom?
- How could you provide more challenge for some learners without giving them more work or a mentoring role?
- How could you provide more support for some learners without altering the assignment?

ISTE Standards for Educators and Variability

The concept of learner variability is explicitly mentioned in Standard 5 of the ISTE Standards for Educators (2017). This standard encourages educators to use technology to personalize the learning experience in order to accommodate learner differences and needs (Indicator 5a). This personalization can be accomplished through a variety of means, from the use of assistive technologies to the inclusion of adaptability features for content. The use of the text-to-speech feature now built into most operating systems is an example of the former, while the ability to adjust the level of complexity of the text (leveling) is an example of the latter. For more information, please see our article, "30+ Tools for Diverse Learners" (**bit.ly/DiveIntoUDLCh5b**).

Pause and Reflect

We believe it is important for all learners (including us) to recognize how to customize our own learning environment. This not only supports your learning needs and preferences, but also helps you better understand the needs and preferences of your learners. To that end, consider:

- What role do you think educators play in helping students customize their learning environment?
- What barriers to learning do these tools remove? What barriers do they add?
- In what ways do you customize your learning environment?
- Are there any ways you haven't tried yet?

Assumption 6: Intentionally Develop Learner Expertise

Although designing more accessible learning environments that account for our learners' variability is a key goal of UDL, it is just one step toward realizing a greater vision: *a more equitable future where every learner has the opportunity to become an expert learner and develop his or her full potential.* Does that statement intimidate you? You are not alone! It can be overwhelming to think about the big picture, especially when most of your day-to-day work focuses more on the details.

Meyer, Rose, and Gordon (2014) describe an expert learner as: purposeful and motivated, resourceful and knowledgeable, and strategic and goal-directed. Because this definition of learning expertise is a somewhat abstract idea, a great place to start is to look at some examples of expert learners in action. As you read the stories of these expert learners, consider also the skills and habits of mind they possess:

Purposeful and Motivated

Sady Paulson (**sadypaulson.com**) is a video editor from Killdeer, North Dakota. Sady has cerebral palsy and uses the accessibility features of her Mac and iPad to edit her videos. She has two buttons placed on the headrest of her wheelchair, and with these buttons she taps to make selections as a cursor navigates the items on the screen. The process is time-consuming and takes patience, concentration, and effort, but Sady is undeterred. Sady's desire to tell her own story and advocate for her needs as a person with cerebral palsy motivated her to learn video editing, and in 2016 she graduated from Full Sail University with a degree in digital cinematography, a 3.63 GPA, and the Advanced Achievement Award for her class. She was even featured in a video that opened one of Apple's keynote presentations! Expert learners like Sady set challenging, yet personally meaningful, goals. These goals keep them on track as they work to overcome the challenges that come up in their quest to reach high levels of performance in their chosen field, whether it is video editing or mastering calculus. Expert learners bring a "growth mindset" (Dweck, 2006) to the task that keeps them focused on continuous improvement as its own reward. Finally, they are capable of self-regulation, not only keeping negative emotions and self-talk in check during the performance itself, but also bouncing back quickly when things don't go their way by taking a reflective approach that gets them quickly re-focused on what they need to improve to get better.

Resourceful and Knowledgeable

Expert learners don't give up. They continuously work to build and use their knowledge as they creatively find clever ways to overcome problems. When Easton LaChapelle (**theroboarm.com**) was 14 he decided he wanted to create a robotic hand controlled by an electronic glove. Easton, taking on this enormous challenge, turned to sites such as Instructables (**instructables.com**) and Hackaday (**https://hackaday.com**) for inspiration and ideas. He lived in a small town and didn't have access to a university to help him build his designs, so he used everyday items, especially Legos, to help him build his prototypes. After he made his first arm he wanted to make something "bigger, better and more functional." Eventually he used 3-D printers to help him create his next series of prototypes. Easton then turned to increasing what the arm could do. Again, he focused on inexpensive everyday motors, such as dimmer switches, learning how they worked as he built out his arm. When he was done the arm could throw a ball or shake your hand. A chance meeting with a 7-year-old girl whose prosthetic arm cost $80,000 pushed Easton to create a fully functioning arm with wireless control for $400—all by the age of 16.

Easton started his journey because he was curious and bored. Using everyday tools, quickly adopting new technology (like 3-D printing), and pursuing his learning through online forums helped him push the boundaries of what was possible. Although Easton is extraordinary, his resourcefulness and desire to learn is possible for all our students. We can encourage curiosity by helping students find problems they are passionate about. We can create learning environments that encourage students to independently build their knowledge using the tools, resources, and supports available. We can introduce methodologies, such as design thinking, to promote problem solving, prototyping, and iteration. Most importantly, we can give them encouragement to pursue their ideas independently, both inside and outside school.

Strategic and Goal-Directed

Expert learners are able to set achievable goals for themselves and have a plan of action to help achieve them. Mo'Ne Davis is an athlete that set and achieved remarkable goals. At 13, she pitched a shutout game, throwing 70 mph fastballs, and was the first girl to earn a Little League series win. Even with all this fame (she was on the cover of *Sports Illustrated*), her real goal is to play basketball. She constantly challenges herself to become a better athlete, often playing against boys and players older than her. She sets realistic goals, targeting weakness, and practicing every day to develop her skills. K. Anders Ericsson (1993) came up with the term *deliberate practice* to describe the kind of intentional and sustained practice that results in expert levels of performance. With this kind of practice, you don't just "go through the motions" mindlessly repeating the moves required to perform a skill, such as making the shot or solving a math problem. You set a goal

Expert Learning and the ISTE Standards for Students

A number of the ISTE Standards for Students (2016) have expert learning as the ultimate goal or outcome. Under Standard 1 (Empowered Learner) the ability to set personal learning goals and to take a reflective approach to the learning process itself (both listed under Indicator 1a) would also describe a purposeful and motivated learner under the UDL definition of expert learning. Similarly, Standard 3 (Knowledge Constructor) emphasizes the ability to employ effective research strategies to locate information (Indicator 3b), evaluate the accuracy and other characteristics of this information (Indicator 3b), and curate it to show meaningful connections and conclusions (Indicator 3c). All these skills are required to be a knowledgeable and resourceful learner under the UDL definition of expert learning. Finally, Standards 5 (Computational Thinker) and 6 (Creative Communicator) include a number of skills learners need to effectively act upon the world to solve problems as strategic, goal-directed learners, the third aspect of expert learning under the UDL principles.

for each session (mastering a new move, or the application of a new algebra concept), until you build a repertoire of strategies for accomplishing your goal. Because of practice, much of what Mo'Ne does on the field or court is automatic. If she misses a pitch or a shot, she calmly assesses her next move, able to quickly adapt to the rhythm of the game, even when the spotlight is on her. A key goal with UDL is to build learners' repertoires of strategies that will similarly allow them to apply their expertise across a number of domains (subjects or topics).

Pause and Reflect

After seeing young expert learners at work, think about your own expertise as a student and now. In what ways were you then, and are you now, purposeful and motivated, resourceful and knowledgeable, strategic and goal-directed? Did you "naturally" have these skills or were they taught to you? Did you gain them inside or outside school? What motivates you now to develop expertise?

Think about a more equitable future where every learner has the opportunity to become an expert learner and develop his or her full potential. Alone, or in a group, create a list of actionable steps to help embed this message in the language and actions of staff and students.

Think back to our car analogy. Not only is it important for students to have options to personalize their experience and environment, but also, eventually, they need to be given the opportunity to get behind the wheel. This might be short drives at first, but as they gain experience and receive feedback, they can go further faster. Eventually, they can plan their own routes and explore the world, confident they have the skills and tools to help them navigate safely.

To sum up, UDL involves changes in both the learning environment and learners themselves. For the environment, a key goal is to create flexible solutions, similar to the options on a car, that enable everyone to participate in learning. For learners themselves, a key goal is to develop their learning expertise through deliberate and strategic practice, similar to learning to drive a car, that results in improved knowledge of self: self-efficacy, self-determination, and self-regulation.

> ***Tweet:*** A key goal of #UDL is to develop learners' expertise through deliberate and strategic practice that results in improved knowledge of self: self-efficacy, self-determination, and self-regulation. #DiveIntoUDL

Next Steps

At its core, UDL is an approach for designing more flexible learning environments where variable learners can find a better fit between their needs and the affordances of the learning environment. With UDL, this is accomplished through proactive planning and design, rather than left to chance or approached with retrofits. Although designing a more inclusive context for learning is key to UDL, this must be done with one key goal in mind: creating the ideal conditions that allow each and every learner to reach his or her full potential as an expert, lifelong learner.

In the next chapter, you will learn the details of UDL Guidelines, the primary tool for putting this chapter's assumptions about learning into practice. Over the last two decades, CAST has developed these Guidelines to take the implementation of UDL from abstract assumptions and theory to practical steps that result in the kinds of environments where all learners have an opportunity to succeed.

Website Activities

To delve even deeper into this subject, scan the QR code to access additional information, videos, and other digital resources related to this chapter on the companion website.

The UDL Guidelines: Translating Theory to Practice

Chapter 5 explored the key beliefs and assumptions about learners and learning that are at the core of UDL. In this chapter, you will examine the science behind these assumptions and take a close look at the UDL Guidelines. The "Wade In" section concentrates on the roots of UDL: the science behind the brain networks and the accompanying why, what, and how of learning. The "Shallow Swim" section details UDL's three principles—Engagement, Representation, and Action and Expression— and their related guidelines. Finally, the "Deep Dive" section explores the connections across the principles, helping form a conceptual framework to guide large-scale and systemic change. As you'll see, each layer of the UDL Guidelines (across all three principles) creates more inclusive and meaningful learning spaces for all learners. Although UDL is quite a complex topic, at every level of understanding you can make a variety of changes to technology access and use, to your instruction, and to the learning environment that will positively impact your learners, and you.

Wade In: Brain Networks and Related Guidelines

As you have learned, the term *Universal Design for Learning* (UDL) was coined by the Center for Applied Special Technology (CAST) and the philosophy behind it has its roots in the Universal Design movement in architecture (see the "Universal Design" section in Chapter 5). From there, UDL grew as a convergence of developments in public policy, neuroscience, classroom practices, and technology.

UDL Video Lesson

UDL is now explicitly referenced in a number of influential documents that guide the direction of educational practice in the U.S., including the Higher Education Opportunity Act (HEOA) of 2008, the Every Student Succeeds Act (ESSA), the most recent version of the National Education Technology Plan, and the 2017 revision of the ISTE Standards for Educators. If you learn better through videos than reading standards, however, CAST's video "UDL at a Glance" (which you can access through the QR code at the end of this chapter) nicely unpacks the term *Universal Design for Learning.* It focuses on proactive planning for instruction that recognizes the diversity of learners and prepares for these learners at the design stage (rather than reacting to their needs later), ensuring the goals, assessment, methods, materials, and environment are designed to meet the needs of the largest range of learners without "retrofitting" or "accommodations."

Figure 6.1 UDL is founded upon the brain's learning networks: affective, recognition, and strategic.

The science behind UDL relates to the brain's three broad learning networks: affective, recognition, and strategic (Figure 6.1).

Affective Network

The *affective network* is located in the center of the brain and deals with the *why* of learning. This brain network monitors the learner's internal and external environments in order to set priorities for behavior. It determines what a learner finds motivating or threatening in a given learning environment, as well as his or her ability to persist when challenges arise. When a student chooses a book to read based on her interest in the topic, the affective network drives that choice as well as her motivation to continue reading when the content becomes more difficult. By providing supports for this network, you can make it more likely that a learner will achieve the goals of a given learning activity.

In recent years, recognizing that emotions, motivation, and self-regulation underpin all learning, CAST placed greater emphasis on the affective network. One way it did this was by rearranging the UDL Guidelines. The affective network is now addressed under the first UDL principle (Multiple Means of Engagement) (CAST, 2018), which was listed last in previous versions of the Guidelines (see the latest version of the UDL Guidelines at **udlguidelines.cast.org**). Developing students' affective network means more than just "entertaining" them. It also means recognizing that intrinsic motivation and control impact learning and that over time students need to learn to monitor and address these feelings internally rather than rely on external support. By helping students develop proactive skills and strategies, you can ensure they are able to persist with learning when feelings of frustration and stress threaten to derail them from reaching their goals.

> **Tweet:** All of the resources we carefully design to be accessible can be wasted if the learner is not motivated or does not have the skills to leverage those resources to drive their own learning. #DiveIntoUDL

Recognition Network

Located in the back of the brain, the *recognition network* is tuned for recognizing patterns in the information received through the senses. It handles the *what* of learning. This network helps learners identify, organize, and understand information, ideas, and concepts in order to translate them into new knowledge. It helps your students recognize the letters, words, and sentences as they read in order to discern the meaning of the text and the tone and intent of the author, as well as make connections to what is already known or previously read. This ability to recognize patterns differs widely between students. Many learners may need support to account for gaps in their background knowledge, as well as help with the identification and categorization of what they see, hear, and read to help them make meaning out of the new information.

Strategic Network

The *strategic network*, which is located in the front of the brain is involved in directing our purposeful motor responses. It deals with the *how* of learning. This network helps learners plan and organize, and then purposefully act on those plans. This network incorporates both the internal mental processes and the connected motor actions and skills. For example, as students approach the writing of an essay, the strategic network directs both the organization and sequence of their ideas, as well as their hands as they type or write down their thoughts. Learners may need a variety of support to successfully plan and execute tasks that require a certain sequence, structure, or steps, such as essay writing, problem solving, and project planning.

The UDL Guidelines–Brain Networks Connection

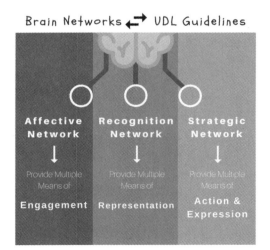

Figure 6.2 The UDL Guidelines principles of Engagement, Representation, and Action and Expression each relate to a specific brain network.

CAST developed the UDL Guidelines to help address variability in learners' brain networks and to help ensure that each learner fully develops their networks for optimal learning (Figure 6.2). When planning for instruction, the UDL Guidelines ask us to stimulate interest and motivation for learning, present information and content in different ways, and differentiate the ways that students can express what they know.

To align with the three brain networks, CAST organized the UDL Guidelines under three broad principles. They are to provide multiple means of:

- Engagement (affective network)
- Representation (recognition network)
- Action and Expression (strategic network)

Engagement

UDL's first principle: Provide Multiple Means of Engagement, refers to how learners are engaged and motivated, Engagement is sectioned into three guidelines. The first is to provide options for *recruiting interest*. Learners may have the same goal, but are offered various options and choices to make the goal relevant and to stimulate each learner's interest. The second guideline is to provide options for *sustaining effort and persistence*. The goal is to help learners develop the ability to maintain both their attention and effort, in order to complete a task or solve a problem successfully. The final guideline is to provide options for *self-regulation*. Over time, we want learners to develop the ability to monitor and successfully manage their internal thoughts and feelings, as well as their external behaviors.

The ultimate goal of Engagement is purposeful, motivated learners.

Representation

UDL's second principle: Provide Multiple Means of Representation focuses on the ways information is presented to learners. Representation is comprised of three guidelines. The first is to provide options for *perception*. Learners are provided the same information but in different media and formats to give individual learners options in how they access information. The second guideline is to provide options for *language, mathematical expression, and symbols*. Learners are given alternative means to decode, understand, and use the language of instruction, including math notation and symbols. The final guideline is to provide options for *comprehension*. The goal of this guideline is for learners to be able to understand and use knowledge. Rather than memorize discrete information, for instance, learners need to come to see how the patterns and features connect to form the big picture, making it easier to understand and connect new information in the future.

The ultimate goal of Representation is resourceful, knowledgeable learners.

Action and Expression

UDL's third principle: Provide Multiple Means of Action and Expression focuses on the ways learners demonstrate their knowledge and skills. Action and Expression is divided into three guidelines. The first is to provide options for *physical action*. Learners have the same goals, but are provided different ways to interact with and produce information. The second guideline is to provide options for *expression and communication*. Learners are given a variety of ways to show what they know beyond paper-and-pencil tasks. The final guideline is to provide options for *executive functions*. The goal is for learners to develop purposeful strategies to support their learning, including goal setting, self-reflection, and organizational strategies.

The ultimate goal of Action and Expression is strategic, goal-directed learners.

Interconnections

Although, for ease of analysis, we have presented the three brain networks and the UDL principles that correspond to them separately, learning is much more complex and interactive. The three brain networks are highly interconnected, and small changes in one network can have an influence on the other two. Barriers that make navigating the learning environment and perceiving information more difficult can have a negative influence on the learner's interest and passion for learning. Conversely, all of the resources we carefully design to be accessible can be wasted if the learner is not motivated or does not have the skills to leverage those resources to drive their own learning.

> ***Tweet:*** Barriers that make navigating the learning environment and perceiving information more difficult can have a negative influence on the learner's interest and passion for learning. #DiveIntoUDL

Pause and Reflect

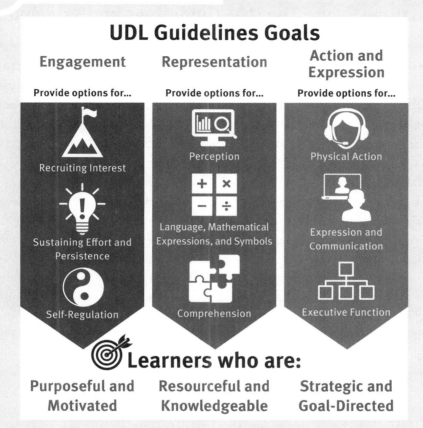

UDL Guidelines Goals

Engagement — Provide options for...
- Recruiting Interest
- Sustaining Effort and Persistence
- Self-Regulation

Representation — Provide options for...
- Perception
- Language, Mathematical Expressions, and Symbols
- Comprehension

Action and Expression — Provide options for...
- Physical Action
- Expression and Communication
- Executive Function

Learners who are:

| Purposeful and Motivated | Resourceful and Knowledgeable | Strategic and Goal-Directed |

Figure 6.3 The three principles of the UDL Guidelines are focused on the goals of UDL.

Think about the three principles that make up the UDL Guidelines (Figure 6.3), their corresponding three networks, and your next lesson. Taking a high-level scan, create a concept map (or any other method of organization, such as a chart or list) and quickly consider what you are currently doing to address the principles as well as some ways you might address them in an upcoming lesson or activity. Also, consider including an additional branch or column to brainstorm possible apps or digital tools that would support the three networks.

Go to the "Next Steps" section (page 108), or continue on to the next level.

Shallow Swim: The UDL Guidelines and Principles

Now that you are familiar with the UDL Guidelines, let's unpack them a bit further to see how each impacts the classroom environment and instructional practices. Each principle is broken down into three guidelines with two to five checkpoints. Consider these checkpoints as actionable steps. Over time, the goal is to shift from adding UDL "components" to your lessons, to embedding UDL into your practice, so it becomes a positive version of TTWWADI (that's the way we've always done it). The UDL Guidelines are not meant to be used as a checklist. Instead, they are meant to be a heuristic, a tool for reflection, decision-making, and instructional design. Rather than attempting to include each guideline and checkpoint in your lesson or unit of study, which can be overwhelming, the goal at this stage is to simply *consider* each guideline and checkpoint, to help ensure you are not overlooking any aspect of UDL just because it is different from the way you have done things in the past. In that way, the UDL Guidelines are a tool for helping you stretch your practice in the classroom, by helping you consider aspects of instructional design you may have otherwise overlooked out of habit.

An example of an ingrained practice that has little evidence to support it is that of designing educational experiences based on learning styles. As Tesia Marshik pointed out in her TEDx Talk (2015) "Don't Believe Everything You Think: Learning Styles and the Importance of Critical Self-Reflection," research questions the use of learning styles as a basis for instructional design, yet the concept continues to be popular among educators. Marshik shared studies that show teaching to different "styles" does not improve learning. Learners are diverse, and learning is a much more complex, and meaning-based task. UDL is designed to support this complexity and variability. As such, learners are exposed to a number of options that accommodate their preferences and strengths, as well as support or scaffold their challenges. When used as a blueprint for instructional design, the UDL Guidelines (CAST, 2018) ensure we are basing our instructional decisions on evidence-based best practices and sound research from the learning sciences. As a reference, the sections that follow summarize each checkpoint. A detailed set of the guidelines is available on the CAST website.

Multiple Means of Engagement

In prior versions of the UDL Guidelines, Engagement and the affective network were listed last. As ongoing research continued to provide insights into the importance of motivation, persistence, and self-regulation for

Universal Design for Learning
Provide Multiple Means of **Engagement**

Provide Options for Recruiting Interest
- Optimize individual choice and autonomy
- Optimize relevance, value, and authenticity
- Minimize threats and distractions

Provide Options for Sustaining Effort and Persistence
- Heighten salience of goals and objectives
- Vary demands and resources to optimize challenge
- Foster collaboration and communication
- Increase mastery-oriented feedback

Provide Options for Self-Regulation
- Promote expectations and beliefs that optimize motivation
- Facilitate personal coping skills and strategies
- Develop self-assessment and reflection

The goal is to develop purposeful, motivated learners.

Figure 6.4 Multiple Means of Engagement includes three guidelines with several checkpoints each.

Engagement in the ISTE Standards

An Engaged Learner is also an Empowered Learner, according to Standard 1 of the ISTE Standards for Students (2016). He or she sets personal learning goals (Indicator 1a) that are both challenging and personally meaningful, then summons both internal and external resources in order to accomplish those goals. Such a learner takes a growth mindset and seeks (rather than avoids) feedback to improve (Indicator 1c). This feedback along with ongoing reflection on the learning process itself (Indicator 1a) keep this learner focused on the ultimate goal: getting better at learning itself rather than just acquiring knowledge.

Tweet: An Engaged Learner is an Empowered Learner: Highly engaged and motivated learners find ways to get around barriers they might encounter, learners with low engagement will stop at even the smallest setbacks. #DiveIntoUDL

learning, CAST revised the Guidelines to reflect those findings. The UDL principle of providing multiple means of Engagement now appears first, before Representation, and Action and Expression (Figure 6.4). Highly engaged and motivated learners who are self-reflective and self-regulatory, will find ways (often creative ones) to get around the barriers they might encounter, while learners with low engagement, motivation, or self-regulation will stop at even the smallest setbacks.

Recruiting Interest

The first guideline of the Engagement principle is to provide options for recruiting learner interest. The UDL Guidelines further break it down into three checkpoints:

- **Optimize individual choice and autonomy**. Provide students with choices—in the tools they use, the ways they demonstrate learning, and where and how they work (individually, in small groups and so on)—and encourage them to actively participate in the design of those choices.

- **Optimize relevance, value, and authenticity**. Provide students with tasks, questions, and problems that tackle big ideas and essential questions that are personally important and bring the relevance, value, and authenticity to learning students crave—and UDL recommends.

- **Minimize threats and distractions**. Create a physically and emotionally safe space in which learners themselves can discover their preferred levels of novelty and sensory stimulus.

Sustaining Effort and Persistence

The second guideline of the Engagement principle is to provide options for sustaining effort and persistence in learners. CAST provides four checkpoints for this guideline:

- **Heighten salience of goals and objectives**. Share lesson goals and objectives often and encourage students to set their own goals to match their growing skills and awareness of their learning needs.

- **Vary demands and resources to optimize challenge**. Provide a balance of structured and more open-ended assignments that challenge students to stretch their skills and ability, and not just "coast."

- **Foster collaboration and communication**. Create collaborative learning groups with clear goals, roles, and responsibilities and encourage students to seek their peers as additional sources of support for their learning.

- **Increase mastery-oriented feedback**. Provide feedback that focuses on growth and improvement (formative assessment) rather than a fixed performance (summative assessment), especially for those learners who see themselves as limited by their learning differences.

Self-Regulation

The third and final guideline of the Engagement principle is to provide learners options for self-regulation. The three checkpoints for this guideline are:

- **Promote expectations and beliefs that optimize motivation**. Support learners' development of a growth mindset (Dweck, 2006) by providing timely feedback that recognizes both their effort as well as their successful application of a variety of learning strategies.

Pause and Reflect

We often talk about motivation, effort, and persistence, but we usually do so in the context of our external role with learners. We don't often discuss how these skills are internalized and how we can develop them (or include them in our instruction). Take a few minutes to reflect on how you are best motivated to learn:

- Do you prefer to work in a group or work individually?
- Do you prefer to listen to music as you study or work, or do you prefer an environment that is clear of distractions, including music and other noise?
- Do you struggle to get started or complete activities, or are you able to quickly organize yourself and get started?
- How do you react to something that is challenging— physically, academically, mathematically?
- When was the last time you got feedback that you could act upon? How did this help you learn?

If you are following along with a group of teachers, ask the other members of your group these questions. How do you differ from them? How are you similar?

- **Facilitate personal coping skills and strategies**. Use prompts and other supports to help learners manage frustration and develop a more positive self-talk when they encounter challenges.

- **Develop self-assessment and reflection**. Build in opportunities for students to pause and reflect on their learning at multiple points in the learning process and use a variety of aids to help them independently monitor their progress toward completion of the key tasks.

Multiple Means of Representation

As Tesia Marshik explained in her TEDx Talk (2015), the learning sciences provide little evidence for the idea of learning styles. Instead, a number of factors play a significant role in how well learners are able to make use of new information to build knowledge (Figure 6.5). One of these factors is how meaningful the information is to the learner. We are more likely to remember a story than a list of facts, for instance. The story provides a familiar structure (beginning, middle, and end) that helps us organize the information. The story may also help us remember the information by relating it to our own experiences so that it is more personally relevant and meaningful.

Another factor in helping us process information is the fit between the nature of the content to be learned and the format selected for presenting it. As Luis himself can attest from his experience trying to learn how to swim as an adult, it is difficult to learn how to swim just by reading about it or watching a video. Practicing the actual strokes in the pool becomes important. However, even with a hands-on skill such as swimming, using a smartphone to record himself while he does each stroke has helped Luis become more aware of his technique and resulted in faster progress. Likewise, presenting lesson information in a variety of modalities in the classroom provides more opportunities for learners to identify the key patterns and relationships they need for comprehension.

Universal Design for Learning
Provide Multiple Means of Representation

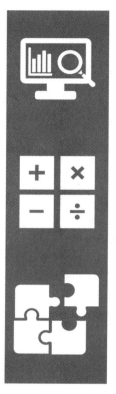

Provide Options for Perception
- Offer ways of customizing the display of information
- Offer alternatives for auditory information
- Offer alternatives for visual information

Provide Options for Language, Mathematical Expressions, and Symbols
- Clarify vocabulary and symbols
- Clarify syntax and structure
- Support decoding text, mathematical notation, and symbols
- Promote understanding across languages
- Illustrate through multiple media

Provide Options for Comprehension
- Activate or supply background knowledge
- Highlight patterns, critical features, big ideas, and relationships
- Guide information processing, visualization, and manipulation
- Maximize transfer and generalization

The goal is to develop resourceful, knowledgeable learners.

Figure 6.5 Multiple Means of Representation includes three guidelines with several checkpoints each.

Perception

The first guideline of the Representation principle is to provide options to account for learners' variability in how they perceive information. The UDL Guidelines further break it down into three checkpoints:

- **Offer ways of customizing the display of information**. Present the information in a format that allows learners to personalize their experience of the content by adjusting the text size, fonts, color, and other visual display options, as well as the pace of presentation.

- **Offer alternatives for auditory information**. Make sure that videos include closed captions and that audio recordings have an associated transcript to make the content accessible to those with auditory difficulties.

- **Offer alternatives for visual information**. Provide text alternatives for images and use physical objects (including 3-D printed models) to make visual information accessible to learners with visual impairments.

Language and Symbols

The second guideline of the Representation principle is to provide options for learners' variability in how they process information encoded in print as well as mathematical notation and other special symbols. CAST provides five checkpoints for this guideline:

- **Clarify vocabulary and symbols**. Pre-teach new vocabulary and special symbols that may be unfamiliar to learners, and embed vocabulary supports in the content through hyperlinked definitions and explanations that are available to learners on demand.

- **Clarify syntax and structure**. Use highlighting, diagramming, and other techniques to take apart a whole (a sentence or a math expression) into its constituent parts (the parts of speech or individual math symbols), and draw attention to the key relationships.

- **Support decoding text, mathematical notation, and symbols**. Allow learners to use text-to-speech technology or audiobooks when the ability to decode words, numbers, or symbols is not the central goal of the activity.

- **Promote understanding across cultures**. Provide translations in the languages spoken in your classroom, embed visual, non-linguistic supports for key vocabulary, and teach learners how to access online translation tools and multilingual dictionaries.

- **Illustrate through multiple media.** Use illustrations, diagrams, animations, and other media to reinforce the concepts presented in text.

Comprehension

The third and final guideline of the Representation principle is to provide learners options for comprehension. The four checkpoints for this guideline are:

- **Activate or supply background knowledge**. Use advanced organizers (such as a Know-Want to Know-Learned or KWL Chart) as well as personal reflection to help learners identify what

Representation in the ISTE Standards

As ISTE Standards for Students (2016) emphasizes in Standard 3, learners with well-developed recognition networks are Knowledge Constructors. They build their knowledge base through the resourceful use of technology to effectively locate information (Indicator 3a) and carefully curate it into collections that demonstrate meaningful connections and conclusions (Indicator 3c) by critically evaluating it for accuracy, perspective, credibility, and relevance (Indicator 3b). They then use this information to build new knowledge to actively explore solutions to real-world issues and problems (Indicator 3d).

Tweet: Both #UDL and ISTE Standards for Students emphasize the active construction of knowledge over the passive consumption of information. #DiveIntoUDL they already know about a new topic, then use analogies and metaphors (such as our swimming example) to relate new information to that which is already familiar.

- **Highlight patterns, critical features, big ideas, and relationships.** Cue learners to identify the main ideas and key relationships in the content through the use of aids such as outlines, concept maps, and other graphic organizers.

Pause and Reflect

In Tesia Marshik's TEDx Talk (2015), she discussed the power of storytelling for memory and learning. When dealing with all the UDL checkpoints under each guideline, it can become overwhelming to think about and apply them. Let's use story to better understand each guideline.

In role, recount your day (or period) as one of your students. Focus your retelling on Representation. (You can always repeat the activity for Engagement and Action and Expression.) Feel free to reference the guidelines and checkpoints as you tell your story:

- Are your perception needs being met? What works for you? What is frustrating?
- Do you have the support you need for language, mathematical expression, and symbols? Are there cultural barriers? Do you need digital access?
- How is your comprehension supported? Do you need more support or practice to build background knowledge, see patterns and relationships, or apply your learning to new problems and situations?

UDL isn't about creating an individual program for each student. As such, think about, or better yet discuss with a colleague, how any changes to support for one student could benefit many, or even all, students in your class.

- **Guide information processing, visualization, and manipulation.** Use descriptive section headings to "chunk" information and reveal its organization to learners.

- **Maximize transfer and generalizability.** Use mnemonic strategies (such as PEMDAS to remember the order of operations in math expressions) to help learners recall information as they practice applying what they have learned in new contexts (including real-world situations).

Multiple Means of Action and Expression

Difficulties with the strategic network often skew the results of assessments that rely on only one means for response. For example, if you struggle with typing, you might find it difficult to complete a timed assessment that asked you to only write responses to an essay prompt. The results of this assessment would confuse your level of understanding of the content with your inability to type and respond within a given amount of time. The UDL principle of providing multiple means of Action and Expression urges us to separate the goals of a lesson from the means for demonstrating understanding whenever possible. For the timed essay, for example, you could allow learners to record their responses in a video if the goal of the lesson was to see how well they understand the key ideas covered in the lesson, not their ability to type or compose an essay. Varying the method for response would not only provide you with a more accurate assessment of each learner's understanding, it would also provide opportunities for learners to expand their repertoire of tools and strategies they can use to support their future learning (Figure 6.6).

Physical Action

The first guideline of the Action and Expression principle is to provide options for how learners physically interact with the learning environment. The UDL Guidelines further break it down into two checkpoints:

Universal Design for Learning
Provide Multiple Means of Action and Expression

Provide Options for Physical Action
- Vary the methods for response and navigation
- Optimize access to tools and assistive technologies

Provide Options for Expression and Communication
- Use multiple media for communication
- Use multiple tools for construction and composition
- Build fluencies with graduated levels of support for practice and performance

Provide Options for Executive Function
- Guide appropriate goal setting
- Support planning and strategy development
- Facilitate managing information and resources
- Enhance capacity for monitoring progress

The goal is to develop strategic, goal-directed learners.

Figure 6.6 Multiple Means of Action and Expression includes three guidelines with several checkpoints each.

- **Vary the methods for response and navigation**. Allow learners to choose from a variety of methods for how they respond, such as by writing their answers down on paper, typing them on a computer or mobile device, or using voice recognition technology to dictate their answers.

- **Optimize access to tools and assistive technologies.** Make sure learners can interact with the software, apps, and other tools used in the classroom with a variety of input methods, including: mouse, keyboard, touchscreen gestures, voice-recognition technology, and switch-access devices.

Action and Expression in the ISTE Standards

The third principle of UDL focuses on the strategic use of new knowledge to purposefully act on the world. A number of ISTE Standards for Students (2016) have a similar emphasis on learners acting strategically to solve problems. For example, as Innovative Designers, learners will use a deliberate design process to generate ideas for solving authentic problems (Indicator 4a), as well as to develop, test, and refine prototypes as part of a cyclical design process (Indicator 4c). As Computational Thinkers, they will use algorithmic (strategic) thinking to explore and find solutions as well as create and test automated solutions (Indicators 5a and 5d). As Creative Communicators, they will then strategically choose the appropriate platforms and tools for sharing their findings and solutions (Indicator 6a) so that they can be implemented more widely and have a greater impact.

Tweet: Providing learners with choice for how they demonstrate understanding results in more accurate assessments of their progress; it also builds their ability to use a variety of tools to support their future learning. #DiveIntoUDL

Expression and Communication

The second guideline of the Action and Expression principle is to provide options for learners' variability in how they express their understanding using a variety of tools and formats. CAST provides three checkpoints for this guideline:

- **Use multiple media for communication.** Unless the use of a particular media is critical to the goal, allow learners to have a choice in the media they use to communicate their understanding: text, speech (presenting in class or an audio recording), video, artwork, a re-enactment of a historical event, and so on.

- **Use multiple tools for construction and composition.** Teach and encourage the use of a variety of supports built into the devices many learners already own: spell checkers, dictionaries, word prediction, text to speech, voice recognition, and more.

- **Build fluencies with graduated levels of support for practice and performance.** Expose learners to a variety of examples that show them how the same goal can be accomplished with a variety of different approaches, then provide ample opportunities for learners to practice and refine their new skills with varying levels of support that lead to more independent performance over time.

Executive Functions

The third and final guideline of the Action and Expression principle is to provide learners with options for their executive functions, the set of skills involved in setting goals and making plans for accomplishing them. The four checkpoints for this guideline are:

- **Guide appropriate goal setting.** Guide learners in setting challenging yet achievable goals that extend beyond the objectives of the current lesson and involve their own growth and development as lifelong learners.

- **Support planning and strategy development.** Provide project-planning templates that help learners break down a big project into smaller steps, with mutually agreed deadlines for checking on progress and making adjustments to the plan as needed.

- **Facilitate managing information and resources.** Expose learners to a variety of note-taking strategies, and encourage them to use a number of online tools (such as Google Keep or Google Docs) to keep information in a central location that can be accessed from a variety of devices as needed.

Pause and Reflect

When educators consider Action and Expression, the voice and choice aspect of UDL are often the focus (expression and communication). While this guideline is important, it could be argued that executive functions play a more important role in helping learners become strategic and goal-directed. With that in mind, take a moment to consider your executive functions.

Which executive functions are finely honed? Are any of your executive functions less than optimal? What do you do to strengthen them or compensate for them? Do you use technology?

How would you go about introducing your students to the term *executive functions* and the important role they play in the ability to effectively remember, organize, plan, and complete tasks?

- **Enhance capacity for monitoring progress.** Provide ongoing, formative feedback that uses a variety of formats (progress charts, portfolios, before-and-after photos) and sources (self-evaluation guided by a rubric, peer conferences, and more).

Go to the "Next Steps" section (page 108), or continue on to the next level.

Deep Dive: UDL and Today's Learner

A few years ago a modest video by Dr. David Rose, "UDL Guidelines Structure" (2010) fundamentally changed how educators viewed UDL. (You can view the whole video using the QR code at the end of this chapter.) Specifically, he shifted the focus away from working through the guidelines as isolated points on a checklist, towards a more global and interconnected view. In the video, Dr. Rose stressed that each principle—Engagement, Representation, and Action and Expression—starts with external factors at the top and transitions into internal factors at the bottom. He emphasized that the purpose of UDL is to develop expert learners. This goal is supported by what CAST now calls the *Internalize* layer and connects the three guidelines—self-regulation, comprehension, and executive function—into a cohesive whole. (To help visualize this, refer to Figure 6.3.) As Dr. Rose explained, our goals for our learners are that:

> They are in fact able to self-regulate. It's not that they have to be stimulated by the outside world, [but] that they're in charge of how things interest them, what they engage in, and what they're willing to put effort in. Similarly, they comprehend whatever is in front of them, they have good strategies, and they know what to do. And lastly, they have great executive function, they make good plans, set goals for themselves that are appropriate, and monitor their progress. So, this [Internalize layer] is the place that we want to get to, and the other guidelines are in fact really part of getting there.

Tweet: Seeing the UDL Guidelines as a layered progression towards learner expertise moves our thinking away from isolated changes to fundamental shifts in how we teach and students learn. #DiveIntoUDL

In this section, we will further explore the overall themes of each layer of the guidelines as you design instruction that supports learner expertise. This layered orientation of the UDL Guidelines in some ways mirrors the history of UDL. (To view these newly labeled layers [Access, Build, Internalize], visit **udlguidelines.cast.org**.)

Access Layer

Containing the entry points for the Guidelines, the *Access* layer reflects UDL's origins in the Universal Design movement. Here you find the UD in UDL, and the goal of removing barriers to learning that keep learners with disabilities and other special needs from accessing education along with their peers. On this layer, the focus of the guidelines and checkpoints for each principle is primarily on the accessibility of the learning

Universal Design for Learning
Access Layer
Create an accessible classroom
and remove barriers to learning

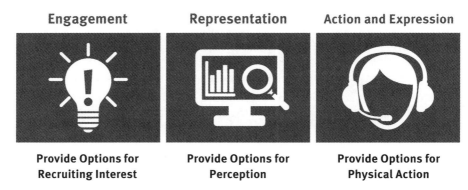

Engagement   **Representation**   **Action and Expression**

Provide Options for **Provide Options for** **Provide Options for**
Recruiting Interest **Perception**   **Physical Action**

Figure 6.7 The Access layer of the UDL Guidelines focuses on creating an accessible classroom and removing barriers to learning.

environment: creating an accessible classroom with options for recruiting interest, perception, and physical action.

The goals of the Access layer are often teacher-driven (Figure 6.7). As you'll explore in subsequent chapters, however, gradual release of responsibility for access can shift to the learner when intentionally planned and explicitly shared with students. In addition, this layer, although not dependent on technology, is certainly expanded through technologies that provide learners with independent options and help "level the playing field."

Without attention to the accessibility of the tools and content we use in the classroom, we cannot realize the goal of making sure the "all learners" part of UDL really does mean *all*. Consider an analogy: Suppose you're a wheelchair user and you want to go for a swim. You enjoy swimming, and as long as you are in the water you can swim just fine. Unfortunately, as you pull up to the building that houses the pool you find that a flight of steep steps is the only way to enter. You might be able to get past this barrier if someone picked you up and carried you inside. As an adult, you probably wouldn't be happy with that solution. When instructional design

Access and the ISTE Standards

Accessibility is explicitly addressed in the new ISTE Standards for Educators (2017). Standard 5 calls for the educator as Designer to use technology to create, adapt, and personalize learning experiences that accommodate learner differences and needs. Similarly, as Leaders, educators are called on to advocate for the equitable access to educational technology, digital resources, and learning opportunities that meet the diverse needs of all students (Indicator 2b)—a very clear statement that aligns the goals of both UDL and the ISTE Educator Standards around equity in education.

Pause and Reflect

Traditionally access to the curriculum has been through print. For many learners information is literally text-bound and inaccessible. Our classrooms reflect this, with the majority of the environment and instruction based on print.

Create an observation list. Spend some time moving about the school recording the number of ways learning is inaccessible to students. What barriers did you discover? What assumptions are behind the current instructional models, tools, or resources? Are the same students affected or a range of students?

In what ways does your school or district encourage learners to personalize their learning through technology? Is the technology available to everyone or only for those in special education? How might you use the technology and resources you currently have to create a more accessible environment?

Figure 6.8 A proactive approach to accessibility benefits everyone.

ignores accessibility, that is in essence what we do: We exclude some learners from the joy of learning available to others. As Figure 6.8 illustrates, good design focuses on usability to ensure the widest range of people can use, and benefit from, the design.

As the entry level of the UDL Guidelines, the Access layer also addresses engagement by pointing out the need to not only recruit the learner's interest but also minimize any distractions. Recruiting interest can be done in a variety of ways: by highlighting the relevance of the content and how it applies to the learner's own life and experience, or by emphasizing choice and autonomy as the learner chooses from a number of options based on his or her own interest and needs. Too often, the introduction of technology is seen as a way to recruit interest, but once the novelty effect wears off so will the superficial engagement that the technology by itself can provide. A more meaningful integration of the technology as a support for more personalized learning, on the other hand, can lead to a deeper and more lasting engagement.

Build Layer

The *Build* layer of the UDL Guidelines is somewhat symbolic of the transition of UDL from an approach that focused primarily on learners "in the margins" of education to one that sought to address the needs of all learners. In this layer, the focus of the guidelines and checkpoints for each principle is primarily on gradually releasing responsibility for learning to learners: giving them the opportunity to set goals, make decisions, and gain a better understanding of how they learn (Figure 6.9). It gives them more autonomy to plan and direct their learning, choosing both the means and methods of demonstrating their growing competencies.

Many educators who are familiar with UDL find it easiest to address the Build layer of the UDL Guidelines in their practices. The focus narrows down to giving students choices in the way they express themselves, often in the form of technology tools that help them construct, compose, and

Universal Design for Learning
Build Layer

**Provide learners with voice and
choice to build learner independence**

Engagement	Representation	Action and Expression

 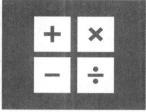 

Provide Options for Sustaining Effort and Persistence	**Provide Options for Language, Mathematical Expressions, and Symbols**	**Provide Options for Expression and Communication**

Figure 6.9 The Build layer of the UDL Guidelines focuses on providing learners with voice and choice to build learner independence.

communicate their learning. Given the wide availability of technology in many classrooms, it is relatively simple to provide learners with a selection of tools they can use to interact with the learning environment and demonstrate their understanding. These may include using Google Slides or Microsoft PowerPoint to create a presentation with visuals to accompany the text, or recording a video using Polished Play's Puppet Pals (**polishedplay.com**) or TouchCast (**touchcast.com**) as an alternative to a more traditional written assignment. The tic-tac-toe option board (Figure 5.7) from Chapter 5, is an example of a simple and effective way to offer students choice through technology selection. Other non-technology ways to increase student ownership include letting students choose the topic they will investigate, the method of organizing and planning, or the final product they will share.

Another relatively easy way to provide students with choice is through online tools with supports for language and communication, such as linking to online glossaries where learners can look up unfamiliar words, using visuals to account for language differences, or selecting tools to aid with translation. The efficiencies technology provides can make a positive difference when matched well with the goals of the learning task. For example, readily available definitions through a built-in glossary can reduce the time it takes to look up unfamiliar words. Sites such as Pixabay (**pixabay.com**) offer a plethora of attribution-free images, and translations offered through a service such as Google Translate can help bridge linguistic barriers.

As the Build layer emphasizes, however, providing the tools is only the first step. Learners need to also understand themselves and the process of decision-making to make informed decisions based on need, not just preference. Moving beyond simple "you decide" choices and including students in the goal-setting process are important steps in helping them grow as independent learners. This can be done in many ways. For example, give them opportunities to reword curriculum goals into student-friendly language, work in collaborative groups to break down long-term goals into actionable parts, and model how to visualize and verbalize what success will look like. This empowers learners, moving them past simple preference-based choice to understanding what they need to do, the options they have, and how each supports their goals and needs. Rather than use technology tools that help you *organize* students (such as reminder apps), instead provide scaffolds to help students use simple calendar tools or goal-setting apps, and learn to independently take responsibility for determining and meeting deadlines.

To further address this layer's guidelines and checkpoints, we can also take advantage of the network effect. We can create virtual communities where learners themselves can support each other instead of relying on only the instructor for feedback and support. One great example of this type of environment is in Google Docs, where learners can review and comment on each other's work in real time. When educators provide students with sentence starters and feedback ideas, as well as monitoring and supporting

> *Tweet:* Moving beyond simple "you decide" choices and including students in the goal-setting process are important first steps in helping them grow as independent learners. #DiveIntoUDL

peer comments within Google Docs, learners will gain valuable skills and strategies to help them sustain their efforts and persist as challenges, which are a natural part of learning, arise.

As with much of UDL, not all of the Build layer requires the use of technology. Sometimes, just a quick reminder of the goal of the activity or timely feedback that encourages a much needed course correction, can make a big difference. Overall, the goal is to shift the learning environment from one that is primarily teacher-driven to one that is increasingly learner-centered and learner-driven. However, this process has to be scaffolded. Learners may begin by examining a number of exemplars that show different ways to successfully complete an activity, then practice creating their own versions of these models with graduated levels of support that fade away as their capabilities grow and they are able to do the activity on their own. Lev Vygotsky, the Russian psychologist, described this process as working in the "proximal zone of development," that area where learners are working on skills that are too difficult for them to complete independently but can be done with help from a more skilled other person (see Chapter 3 for fuller discussion of this concept). With UDL, that other person can and should be a more skilled peer or an online resource, not just the teacher.

Collaborative Voices in the ISTE Standards

The ISTE Standards for Educators (2017) rethink the role of the educator into that of a Facilitator who models creativity and creative expression (Indicator 6d), fosters a culture where learners take ownership of learning (Indicator 6a), uses collaborative tools to expand learning opportunities by making connections (sometimes virtually) to experts, peers, and community members (Indicator 4c), and uses cultural competency to ensure the voices of all learners are heard (Indicator 4d). By modeling collaboration with our fellow educators, parents, and learners themselves, we empower learners and support change. We signal we are ready and willing to give our students the wheel, and take a seat as willing passengers.

Universal Design for Learning
Internalize Layer

**Expand learner metacognition,
agency, and ability to think deeply**

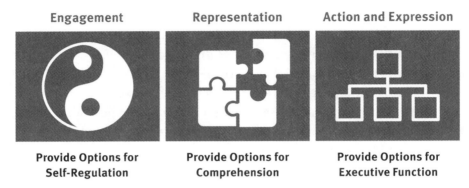

Engagement	Representation	Action and Expression
Provide Options for Self-Regulation	**Provide Options for Comprehension**	**Provide Options for Executive Function**

Figure 6.10 The Internalize layer of the UDL Guidelines focuses on expanding learner metacognition, agency, and the ability to think deeply.

> ***Tweet:*** A key goal with #UDL is the development of the self: expert learners are self-determined, self-motivated, and self-regulating. #DiveIntoUDL

Internalize Layer

Finally, the *Internalize* layer of the UDL Guidelines represents the aspirational goals for UDL's future: developing expert, future-ready learners who are self-regulating, self-directed, and self-actualizing.

As Dr. Rose described in his video, the goal of the Internalize layer of the UDL Guidelines is to create expert, self-regulating learners who can accomplish the learning tasks independently or with minimal prompting and assistance (Figure 6.10). Expert learners are defined as learners who are purposeful and motivated, resourceful and knowledgeable, and strategic and goal-directed. These learners set challenging goals for themselves and approach learning with a growth mindset. In addition to having substantial background knowledge to draw upon, these learners have developed media literacy skills that allow them to effectively acquire, evaluate, and integrate new information into their existing knowledge base. They also have well-developed metacognitive skills, including the ability to monitor their progress, self-assess, and reflect on their own learning. Instead of applying random approaches on the chance that they might work, these learners can draw on a number of strategies and coping skills they have developed through ongoing practice to address both learning and

Pause and Reflect

With a group of educators, watch David Rose's video and consider the following questions:

- What section(s) of the guidelines do you focus on? Why and how?
- What section(s) of the guidelines have you yet to explore deeply? Why?
- What changes about your understanding of UDL when you move from viewing the guidelines "vertically" to a more "layered" approach?
- How can we both embed and model the "internalized" aspect of UDL with our students and as a school/district?
- What aspects of our school/district strategic plan align with the overall goal of UDL: that of learner expertise?

Then, using the "Layer" images from the book (Figures 6.8, 6.9, and 6.10) as well as the newly revised UDL image (available from **udlguidelines .cast.org**), work together to:

1. Create a collaborative definition for each layer: Access, Build, Internalize. What does this mean for your school/district?
2. Explore next steps by highlighting the following for each of the three layers: What are we currently doing? What do we envision for our learners? How will we get there? This can be done as SMART goals or a Gantt Chart, or by using an online tool such as Trello (**www.trello.com**).

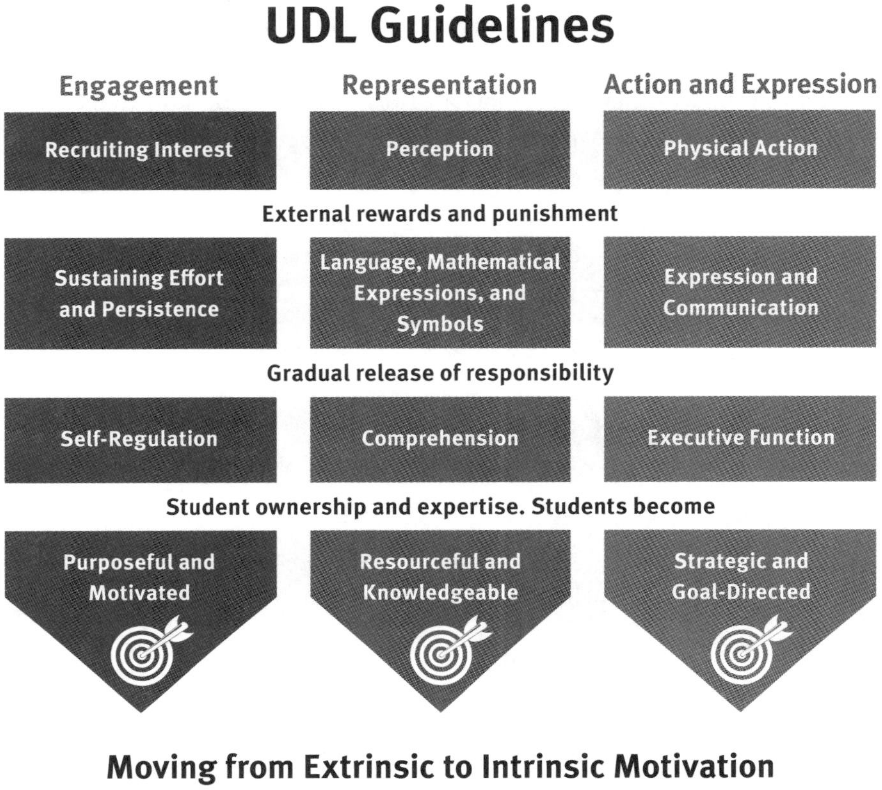

UDL Guidelines

Engagement	Representation	Action and Expression
Recruiting Interest	Perception	Physical Action

External rewards and punishment

Sustaining Effort and Persistence	Language, Mathematical Expressions, and Symbols	Expression and Communication

Gradual release of responsibility

Self-Regulation	Comprehension	Executive Function

Student ownership and expertise. Students become

Purposeful and Motivated	Resourceful and Knowledgeable	Strategic and Goal-Directed

Moving from Extrinsic to Intrinsic Motivation

Figure 6.11 The UDL Guidelines help move the classroom from teacher-directed instruction, defined by extrinsic control and motivation, to student-driven learning, defined by internal control and motivation.

emotional challenges they might encounter. In short, expert learners are self-determined learners who take full ownership of their own learning.

Next Steps

Regardless of where you are in your understanding, exploration, and application of UDL, consider thinking about the UDL Guidelines as a continuum that starts with external factors in the environment and moves inward to more internal factors that reside in the learner.

Consider each column of Figure 6.11. More specifically, think of the Engagement principle in terms of starting at the top with motivation as extrinsic motivating factors (encouragement and support from an external other) and transitioning down to internal motivating factors (the learner's own drive and desire to learn). Together, these principles support the goal of engagement: the development of purposeful, motivated learners. These learners approach learning tasks with curiosity and excitement, and they find joy in learning.

Think of the Representation principle in terms of access to information, moving from the external presentation of information (teacher provided tools and resources that meet a variety of needs) down to understanding of information (the learner is able to comprehend, see critical features, and make sense of what they see, hear, and read). Together, the guidelines for this principle support the goal of representation: the development of resourceful, knowledgeable learners.

Think of the Action and Expression principle in terms of strategies for learning, moving from the external options and choice (the teacher provides a variety of tools and options for learners to express what they know) down to internal goal setting, strategies, and understanding of self (the student is metacognitive and can independently choose goals and strategies to move their learning forward). Together, these guidelines in the Action and Expression principle support the goal for action and expression: the development of strategic, goal-directed learners. These learners understand themselves and know how they learn best.

Taken together, this focus helps us move—from extrinsic to intrinsic, from teacher-driven instruction to student-driven learning—to help us achieve the ultimate goal of UDL: developing expert learners who are purposeful and motivated, resourceful and knowledgeable, and strategic and goal-directed.

At this point, you should have a deeper understanding of the assumptions supporting the adoption of UDL and the UDL Guidelines that were developed to guide its implementation, but you may still have a lingering question: What does it look like in the classroom? Don't worry. In Part 3, we will provide you with examples of how to approach the redesign of a traditional lesson to better incorporate the principles and guidelines of UDL. Read on to see UDL in action, or scan the QR code to access the resources and activities on the companion website.

Website Activities

Pause and Reflect

Transferring ownership of learning to students is a subtle and nuanced experience. Limited "you decide" choices, such as determining the app they can use to complete a task or picking an essay topic from a list, only scratches the surface. Some challenges to increasing student independence and ownership of their learning are system barriers, such as prescribed curriculum, testing, reporting, and grades, as well as educator resistance to shifting and sharing control.

Consider completing an ownership audit, using a chart, similar to Figure 6.12.

Growing Student Ownership	System Barriers We Encounter	Resistance to "Loss of Control"	Ideas for Shared Ownership	Teaching and Transferring
Goal Setting				
Supports for Comprehension				
Construction and Expression				

Figure 6.12 Use this chart to create a high-level view of the barriers to student ownership, as well as to brainstorm ways to increase shared ownership in your class or school.

Use the chart to explore with other educators the barriers they see and the resistance they feel towards co-owned learning environments. Then brainstorm ideas to increase the shared level of ownership and define how ownership can be scaffolded and transferred.

PART
3

Inquire, Plan,
Act, Reflect

Introduction to the Lesson Makeover

O ur goal for Part 3 of this book is to demonstrate how even a traditional lesson can be redesigned (and then transformed) through the intentional application of UDL. We will examine a solid science lesson for evidence of UDL, and then, over the next three chapters, give it a makeover based on the three levels of UDL understanding: Wade In, Shallow Swim, and Deep Dive.

As you explore ways to clear a path for all learners, it is important to give yourself time to integrate what you learn into your practice. As you thoughtfully and intentionally apply UDL strategies, you should feel positive that every change you make, no matter how small, will benefit your learners.

You don't have to change everything about your instruction overnight. We recommend taking small steps, knowing there is more, but feeling confident that the changes you are implementing will positively impact learners. Think of it as setting a goal to swim 30 laps in a pool. If you do too much too soon, you'll most likely give up, exhausted and frustrated. To avoid an "all or nothing" mindset, the three stages of our swimming analogy were designed as a means to help you monitor your professional growth over time and to provide guidance and insight as you apply the deeper aspects of UDL to your practice.

Variability, Inquiry, Ownership, Metacognition

Remember that developing expertise in UDL isn't merely a matter of working your way through each principle's guidelines like a to-do checklist. UDL isn't a "program" with step-by-step instructions, but rather a framework and a mindset. UDL asks us to accept responsibility for our role in creating "disabling" learning environments, and to proactively work towards creating more inclusive ones. Understanding the *why* behind the UDL changes you are making (and seeing the benefit for learners) is more important than charging through the stages to become an "expert."

Avoiding UDL Implementation Pitfalls

Although the guidelines and principles immediately make sense to most educators, full implementation of UDL is often elusive. We see two main reasons for this: viewing the UDL Guidelines as a menu of choices and focusing too tightly on instructional design alone.

Menu Options

Educators fall into a menu mindset and treat the Guidelines as a menu with nine separate options to choose among rather than a cohesive whole. This approach is more like a Whac-A-Mole game, reactively applying UDL to problems as they pop up, rather than following a proactive planning process (Figure 7.1). The Whac-A-Mole method ignores the hierarchical design of the guidelines, the interconnections between principles, and the ultimate goal of UDL: learner expertise. Often it results in educators narrowing their focus down to providing students with options and choice in how they demonstrate their learning but little else. Although this is a good way to wade in, implementation shouldn't stop here. Ensuring learners have barrier-free access to information and learning, supporting the process of learning, and helping students develop learner expertise are far more challenging and equally important goals.

Figure 7.1 Instead of the Whac-A-Mole game of reacting to learning challenges as they pop up, proactively plan for variability and inclusion with UDL.

Instructional Design

Another method of implementation focuses on analyzing instructional goals, methods, materials, and assessments with a UDL lens. This approach can be an effective way to wade in, but, like the menu mindset, it has pitfalls. For example, it is possible to add a variety of UDL components into instruction following this method and still have a very traditional classroom where the teacher makes most of the important decisions, is the only assessor, and maintains extrinsic control through rewards and punishment. Following this approach, educators often struggle to determine the next steps and fail to take a deeper dive into such questions as:

- How does goal setting (instructional and personal) change as students take ownership of their learning?
- How do I take on the role of co-learner without relinquishing my responsibilities as a teacher?
- How do I define assessment, and what is its purpose in a learner-driven environment?
- How do I develop student metacognition, and where does it fit in my instruction?

SWIM: Start Where I aM

The menu and instructional design implementation methods tend to be augmentative approaches rather than transformative ones. Without intent, UDL becomes an add-on rather than a game changer. As we've discussed, the need to create a very different classroom for a very different learner is paramount. Both the UDL Guidelines and the ISTE Standards for Students (2016) and Educators (2017), emphasize (and help you prepare for) the many fundamental shifts happening in education. To this end, we created the UDL and ISTE Standards Crosswalk (**DiveIntoUDL.com**). In this document you can take a deeper dive exploring how all three documents encourage and support shifts in instructional design, deep learning and inquiry, and ownership of learning.

UDL implementation should be viewed as a spiral, allowing you to go deeper as you explore each level. To help begin the iterative process of implementing the UDL Guidelines, ask yourself three questions:

- How do I apply UDL principles in strategic and intentional ways in order to examine their effect on my learners and my practice?
- How do I shift from print-based instruction as the benchmark and leverage technology to ensure learning is accessible in my classroom?
- How will my instructional design and classroom environment change as I introduce students to, and help them develop, learner expertise?

To help you answer these questions, we created the UDL Planning Guide, which is designed to provide you with the big picture and also act as a detailed planner with actionable next steps for implementation. To illustrate the big picture, the UDL Planning Guide focuses three categories or domains to support the creation of a UDL classroom: Flexible Instructional Design, Deep Inquiry and Understanding, and Ownership of Learning (Figure 7.2). Within these, the Planning Guide then provides actionable steps for each area of focus. Throughout, the Planning Guide incorporates the principles and goals of UDL as well as the higher order thinking skills, global competencies, understanding of self, and habits of mind required of today's learners.

Here's a quick overview of what the Planning Guide includes:

Flexible Instructional Design Category

- Category Goal: Intentionally create flexible, open learning experiences and environments that celebrate and plan for learner variability.
- Focuses on:
  - › Learner Variability
  - › Instructional Goals
  - › Accessible Materials, Resources, and Tools
  - › Instructional Methods
  - › Formative Assessment and Feedback

UDL PLANNING GUIDE

- **Flexibility**
- **Inquiry**
- **Ownership**

Using an iterative inquiry approach, the goal is to build inclusive classrooms designed to support, enhance, and accelerate learner expertise.

Flexible Instructional Design

Intentionally create flexible, open learning experiences and environments that celebrate and plan for learner variability.

Deep Inquiry and Understanding

Provide opportunities for learners to develop the skills, strategies, and habits of mind to explore personally meaningful questions and problems deeply with others.

Ownership of Learning

Provide ongoing opportunities for learners to build metacognition, self-regulation with the necessary skills and habits to successfully drive their own learning.

Figure 7.2 The synergy between the three implementation domains (on the right) results in a UDL classroom where learners develop expertise and drive their own learning.

> › Physical Environment
> › Social Environment

Deep Inquiry and Understanding Category

- Category Goal: Provide opportunities for learners to develop the skills, strategies, and habits of mind to explore personally meaningful questions and problems deeply with others.
- Focuses on:
  - › Authentic Learning Opportunities
  - › Deep Comprehension of Concepts and Ideas
  - › Knowledge Curation and Construction
  - › Interdisciplinary Expertise
  - › Open Creation and Communication
  - › Collaborative, Global Citizen

Ownership of Learning Category

- Category Goal: Provide ongoing opportunities for learners to build metacognition, self-regulation, and the necessary skills and habits to successfully drive their own learning.
- Focuses on:
  - › Personal Goal Setting
  - › Learner Voice and Advocacy
  - › Self-Reflection and Metacognition
  - › Executive Function
  - › Self-Monitoring and Self-Regulation
  - › Agency

Lesson Redesign

Throughout the next three chapters we will redesign a traditional lesson, moving from the Wade In to Shallow Swim to Deep Dive levels and referencing the UDL Planning Guide in our changes. We'll then challenge you to use the Planning Guide to think of additional ways to build out UDL elements and grow your practice.

In a sense, you will be deconstructing the lesson in much the same way you would deconstruct a cheeseburger into its various ingredients—meat,

When you deconstruct your lessons to align with UDL Principles, you may need to eliminate some ingredients in favor of new, flavorful ones.

Figure 7.3 Just like your deconstructed lessons, once all the burger ingredients are in front of you, you can decide what to keep and what to change, creating an improved culinary creation, filled with exciting, new ingredients.

cheese, tomato slices, bun, condiments. As you then put the ingredients back together to reconstruct the lesson, you need to keep in mind how the individual components combine and what new ingredients are available to create an appetizing and engaging whole. For instance, the top image in Figure 7.3 shows the basic ingredients that make up a cheeseburger. In the assembled burger, however, you may notice a variety of changes: Some ingredients were left out (purple onions), new ingredients were added (ham), new techniques were used (caramelized onions), and a new sequence was applied (tomato on the bottom). Creating the burger, we realize that some ingredients or methods we may have used in the past no longer work for the new burger we are trying to make. As you redesign your lesson, consider the ingredients you may need to remove or add, as you combine the various components into an appetizing whole.

A UDL lesson is similar in some ways but different in others. Of course, we want to get our learners' attention, and as with a burger, the more appealing or engaging presentation is typically going to do that better than the deconstructed one. We are after a deeper form of engagement, however, one that goes beyond first impressions. This deeper level of engagement comes from work that is personally relevant and meaningful to each learner—giving learners the opportunity to design their own burgers if you will. Approaches such as project-based and challenge-based learning, which engage learners in authentic tasks with room for pursuing their personal concerns and interests, can help provide this level of engagement when viewed through a UDL lens.

From here, you can choose your approach. You can jump directly to the lesson makeover chapter that best matches your needs and interests. Alternately, you may decide to move through each level to view the progression of the lesson as we first add to (make accessible, Chapter 8), then amplify (build skills and provide options and choice, Chapter 9), and finally transform (internalize skills to develop learner expertise, Chapter 10) a highly rated, but traditional, lesson on biomes from PBS Learning-Media (**pbslearningmedia.org**). Our goal is to approach this lesson makeover from the perspective of a "critical friend," providing actionable feedback to make the lesson more effective and relevant for learners. Rather than feel "criticized," we educators should adopt this iterative mindset, recognizing there are always ways to improve our practice.

Next Steps

Before you explore our suggested changes to the lesson, you may want to review it first, determine where the application of UDL is evident, and think about what changes you would make. You can access the link to the lesson at **bit.ly/DiveIntoUDLCh7a**.

Website Activities

If you'd rather study the UDL Planning Guide before moving on, scan the QR code to access it, along with videos, activities, and other interactives on the book's companion site.

Wade In: All-Access Classroom

At the Wade In level of applying UDL, you and your students are exploring and preparing for profound shifts in teaching and learning, in particular changing roles and responsibilities. Changes are subtle but important as you focus on access, awareness building, and classroom culture through the lens of the Access layer of the UDL Guidelines. At this stage, the teacher continues to direct most of the learning, helping students build foundational skills and strategies that underpin their growing responsibility as independent, self-directed learners. To put this in terms of the hamburger analogy: Every learner gets to choose their burger from a variety of premade choices. The teacher explains what is in each burger and ensures a variety is available. The burgers represent good options based on combinations that take into account preferences (vegetarian) and needs (allergies). Students get a choice in what they consume (Figure 8.1).

Figure 8.1 At the Wade In level of implementing UDL, the educator continues to direct most of the learning, such as by providing a range of premade choices.

The Biomes Lesson

At this initial level, you can use a variety of ways to bring simple but effective changes to the classroom through the existing Biomes lesson. Although you could alter many aspects of this lesson, remember that the goal is to take an iterative approach: to narrow your focus and deepen your exploration, rather than go wide and shallow. In this example, we will use the UDL Planning Guide and concentrate on three areas in two categories:

- **Flexible Instructional Design:** Instructional Goals and Accessible Materials, Resources, and Tools
- **Ownership of Learning:** Agency

Instructional Goals

Take a look at the Instructional Goals focus under the Flexible Instructional Design category. (Remember, you can access the pages of the UDL Planning Guide via the QR code at the end of Chapter 7.) From the row's Wade In level, we chose three areas to concentrate on for the Biomes lesson:

- Separate the goal from the means to demonstrate the goal.
- State learning goals in student-friendly language.
- Help learners to articulate the learning goals.

Notice these three points not only help learners understand what is expected of them, but also help them begin to "own" the goals by articulating them. More importantly, by separating goals from means, you've started to move the needle on what learning is and who is successful in demonstrating it.

Next, consider the goals or objectives for the original lesson on biomes:

- Identify terrestrial and aquatic biomes.
- Describe the environmental factors and the plants and animals of each biome.
- Identify the location of different biomes on a world map.
- Understand the interrelationship between environmental factors and the plants and animals within a biome.
- Describe examples of plant and animal adaptations to specific biomes.

Now, ask yourself the following questions for each of the lesson's goals:

1. What kind of goal is it? Is it a content (knowledge) goal that expresses what learners should know? Is it a method (skills) goal that expresses what learners should be able to do?

2. Does the goal separate the ends from the means of achievement? If so, how?

3. If the goal does not separate the ends from the means of achievement, what kinds of scaffolds could I provide to support the learner in achieving the goal?

4. Does the goal state exactly what is expected of students? What is missing?

5. Is the goal in student-friendly language? Could my learners articulate the goal as it is stated? What support would they need? What changes would need to be made?

In the Biomes lesson example, most of the goals focus on what learners should *know* at the end of the lesson, using words such as *identify*, *describe*, and *understand*. From a UDL perspective this is good, because *how* learners identify or describe the environmental factors of each biome or the plants and animals found in it is not specified, and this provides learners with some flexibility for how they can demonstrate their understanding (UDL Guidelines: Optimize choice and autonomy). Take care however, as *describe* often means oral or written language.

The one exception is the third goal, which requires learners to identify the location of different biomes on a world map. During the lesson, a print map is used for this purpose. Such a map, which presents the information using a graphic only, would be inaccessible to a learner who is not able to see it due to a visual impairment. Students who struggle with printed text or have visual processing difficulties will also find the map's information equally inaccessible. In addition, younger students (the lesson is designed for Grades 3–12) may have little conceptual understanding of a world map and as such pointing out biome locations is a visual memory task. The requirement that learners sketch in pencil where they think each biome is located could also create a barrier for learners with difficulties with fine motor skills.

There are two ways you could proceed. First, you could consider if this objective/goal is necessary in order to meet the standards the lesson addresses or is developmentally appropriate. A review of the standards listed for this lesson, including the relevant Next Generation Science Standards, does not reveal any mention of skills related to locating information on a map. Thus, removing the objective/goal would probably not have a negative impact on your ability to meet the stated standards for this lesson. You might also want to consider Wiggins and McTighe's (2005) work on Understanding by Design (UbD), an approach to instructional design that focuses on backward planning around the enduring understandings we want learners to have. They recommend, when planning instruction, determining what is essential, important, and nice to know. *Essential* questions are deep, rich questions. *Nice to know*, like locating something on a map, is a less important skill that may take away from time we could use to focus on the essential skills and concepts related to the main focus, such as the science aspects, of the lesson.

If, however, you determined that the goal is necessary to meet a standard, you would have to use a different kind of map to ensure you are not introducing barriers for some learners. For example, you could use a tactile map, such as the ones provided by the American Printing House for the Blind (APH), and you would just have to account for the cost of this specialized map as well as the time required to acquire it. Although you may not have any blind students in your classroom currently, with the trend toward inclusion, it is possible that you could in the future. Planning for that variability now would make your lesson plan more flexible and reusable in the future, regardless of who comes through the door at the beginning of each school year. Furthermore, a tactile map may be simpler and thus more easily processed by someone whose spatial skills are not as advanced. Thus, the tactile map would be "essential for some, but useful for all."

After revising the goals, they might look as follows. Notice that they are now written from the learner's perspective. They also include specific and measurable criteria and the means to demonstrate understanding is not limited by a narrowly prescribed method.

Pause and Reflect

Before reading our suggestions, take a moment to rewrite the Biomes lesson's goals by separating the goals from the means. Your goals may look different from ours depending on your grade level. To help you focus the goals, consider using the SMART mnemonic. Goals that are Specific, Measurable, Attainable, Results-oriented, and Time-bound are more easily understood and measured. There is a PDF version of a SMART goal planner available for you to use on the book's companion website.

At the end of this lesson, I will be able to:

- Identify my biome type (terrestrial or aquatic) and include three (3) reasons for my identification.
- Describe at least three (3) environmental factors and five (5) native plants and animals of my biome.
- Show my understanding of how environmental factors are interdependent with the plants and animals within my biome.
- Identify at least three (3) similarities and three (3) differences between my own biome and a partner's biome.
- Describe at least three (3) examples of plant and animal adaptations found in my biome.

Once you've separated the goals from the means, focus on helping learners articulate these goals. At this stage, if you usually write goals on the board for students to reference or record, you may want to consider having students work with you to write them in more student-friendly language and/or have students articulate what the goals mean to them. This could be done through a simple think-pair-share where partners talk with each other about the lesson's goals, and then the class shares out what each goal means to them. Or, if you have a survey or questionnaire tool, such as Google Forms or Socrative (**Socrative.com**), you could quickly garner whether students understand the goals or can match the goals with a student-friendly version. This type of task would also serve as a quick formative assessment, helping you gauge student readiness to move forward in the lesson.

Accessible Materials, Resources, and Tools

The second area of focus for this lesson is on accessible materials to present information to learners. Consult the Accessible Materials focus under the Flexible Instructional Design category. From the Wade In level, we chose the following two areas to concentrate on for the Biomes lesson:

- Locate a variety of *accessible* digital, video, visual, and print resources to support access to information, opportunities to interact with the information, and ways to demonstrate the learning.
- Make available, demonstrate, and model the use of technology to support access to, processing of, and demonstration of learning (text-to-speech, screen reader, word prediction, etc.).

This concentration for the lesson is important in four ways:

- Providing a variety of ways to access, engage with, and process information opens doors for learners.

- It is easy to stop at providing "options and choice" and forget to ensure accessibility. Actively engaging with resources to ensure they are accessible to the widest variety of learners gives you insight into the advantages and limitations of the various media.

- Ensuring resources and tools are accessible to all is also an excellent way to walk the UDL talk. It sends a tangible message that the classroom is changing; its positive impact on students is immediate.

- Providing options that include support technology such as text to speech or speech to text, acknowledges the importance of thinking (over decoding or writing) and offers support when goals and means cannot be separated.

Biomes Lesson Materials

The materials for the Biomes lesson include a number of multimedia resources learners will use to research the different biomes as well as worksheets and other tools they will use during a group brainstorming activity. A lesson's materials are one area where the need for accessibility is paramount. The goal with UDL is not just to provide access to information, but also to provide the supports and scaffolds that empower learners to make use of that information in order to turn it into useful knowledge. If there are significant barriers in the materials, however, then the process of turning information into useful knowledge becomes more difficult and engagement can suffer as learners become frustrated by the level of effort required to overcome those barriers.

No one media is perfect for all learners. For this reason, it is important to provide a selection of media and tools for learners to use, taking the time to ensure they are accessible or that technology will allow the learner to interact and learn from them. In the Biomes lesson, a teacher might be

Figure 8.2 No single resource, even if it is digital, is free of barriers. For this reason, it is important to provide a range of options.

tempted to skim the resources and, because they are digital, assume they are accessible. It is important to recognize that it isn't as simple as digital equals accessible equals UDL (Figure 8.2).

Pause and Reflect

Using the QR code at the end of the chapter, go to the Biomes lesson site (**bit.ly/DiveIntoUDLCh7a**) and consider the following questions as you examine the various materials and resources chosen for the Biomes lesson:

- Are there alternatives for visual information? What if a learner has difficulty seeing or processing the information, will he or she still be able to perform the activity?
- Are there alternatives for auditory information? What if a learner has difficulty hearing the information, will he or she still be able to perform the activity?
- Are learners able to customize the display of information (either visually or orally) to accommodate their needs?
- Are there alternatives for how learners can respond and participate in the activity?
- Are there options to support learners' variable understanding of the lesson's key vocabulary, expressions, and symbols?
- Are there options for supporting learners' fluency across languages?

In the "Online Interactive" and "Video" sections, we discuss how we assessed the various resources. Did you see some of the same barriers? Which materials were the most accessible? Which ones would you change?

Online Interactive

The Biomes interactive appears to be an engaging and accessible resource at first glance, but it contains several barriers to its use. At the access level, the interactive was created using Flash, a technology in its waning days, and is not natively supported on some mobile devices such as the iPad.

When the resource does open, it is inaccessible to screen readers, meaning the text is unavailable to some learners. Finally, although not directly related to accessibility, but important as we consider what tools we want to include in the lesson, the activity isn't really interactive. Students click on images to locate text-based information and simple images and diagrams on various biomes.

Consider finding interactive tools that enable students to explore an idea, test their questions, or experience cause and effect, rather than just deliver content in a pretty package. For example, the Missouri Botanical Garden's Biomes of the World site (**mbgnet.net**) is more accessible, and contains the same information as the Biomes lesson's "interactive" one. To engage students in building digital biomes, there are tools like Habitat Maker (**mrnussbaum.com/habitats**) and Mojang's Minecraft (**minecraft.net/en-us**), with which students could build a biome from scratch. You can go to **interactivesites.weebly.com/habitats.html** to compare examples of interactives or use the QR code at the end of the chapter to access them.

Video

One area of accessibility where the Biomes lesson shows exemplary practices is in the inclusion of accessible video as a multimedia resource that learners can use to learn about the different biomes. The videos from PBS LearningMedia are embedded on the website using the JW Player (**www.jwplayer.com/video-solutions/jw-player**), a mobile-friendly option for content creators to deliver Web videos while supporting a number of accessibility features:

- **Closed captions**: These provide the information visually (as text) for learners who are not able to hear the audio in each video. The captions could also help learners with limited vocabulary for this topic as well as English Language Learners. Studies show captions increase all learners' comprehension and retention (Linebarger, 2001; Evmenova, 2008). With the JW Player, the captions can be adjusted to make them easier to read by changing the color and opacity of the text and background, making the text larger, choosing a different font, and more.

- **Keyboard accessibility**: The JW Player can be controlled with a number of simple keyboard shortcuts. For instance, with shortcuts you can play/pause the video, skip forward/back, adjust the volume level by 10% increments, and even start full-screen mode to remove the distractions from the rest of the page.

- **Audio described version**: Audio descriptions explain what is happening in the video to someone who can't see it. The link to a described version of the video is located right below the original version, where it is easy to find on the page.

While the inclusion of captions and audio description is to be lauded, a transcript would also be helpful. A transcript would make the information accessible to someone who is both blind and deaf and who could then use a refreshable Braille display to access the information. Transcripts are also useful for those who prefer to read information or need to reference the information contained in the video quickly. A control for slowing down the rate of the speech and video would be helpful for those learners who process information at a different pace (or who just want to speed up the speaking rate to consume the content when they have limited time). Perhaps the most difficult at this time is providing material in alternate languages. Although sometimes a video is available in other languages, often these resources need to be individually researched and sourced. Translating transcripts is much easier.

Agency

The third area of focus for this lesson's UDL makeover relates to having a choice of accessible materials. In this case, the materials contain information, but their main use is for students to do something with them such as plan, organize, or demonstrate what they know. Giving students only one form of response (such as a printed worksheet) creates a barrier. The student can't demonstrate what they know as they are focused on the motor aspects of the activity. When the inaccessible material is part of group work, it is embarrassing. Often the only role for the student who struggles with a particular media is that of "helper" (or disrupter). When possible include a variety of material options and/or provide technology tools to ensure access and aid completion.

Consult the Agency focus under the Ownership of Learning category. From the Wade In level, we chose the following four areas to concentrate on for the Biomes lesson:

- Give students choice over the type of information resources they access to complete the task.
- Provide students with a variety of materials and methods to demonstrate what they know.
- Provide all students access to and choice of support technology (text to speech, word prediction, concept mapping, and so on).
- Explore and discuss choice and the learner's responsibility to make good choices for their learning and growth.

Biomes Worksheet

The first activity in the Biomes lesson involves a worksheet. When printed, the PDF version of the worksheet is inaccessible to many students, particularly as it has defined areas in which to write. Students with spatial and fine motor issues would find this particularly difficult. If students can work within a digital copy, it should be accessible using a variety of tools including speech to text and text to speech. Just make sure the PDF is readable. Often a PDF is simply an image of the intended document, which means screen readers are unable to read it. Another option, rather than printing the document or having students access it online, would be to create a more accessible digital version using Google Forms or Google Docs. Other options would be for students to create a mind map of the information (which is Kendra's preferred method). This could be sketched or created using online tools or apps such as Inspiration Maps (**inspiration.com/inspmaps**), Ideaphora (**ideaphora.com/our-technology**), or MindNode (**mindnode.com**).

Brainstorming on Chart Paper

A second activity suggested in the Biomes lesson involves students moving around the room in groups recording ideas on chart paper. Rather than creating several paper-based stations, consider providing a variety of media stations, including an interactive station (such as an interactive whiteboard) where students could add pictures or sketch ideas, iPads with a memo or sketchnote app open, a concept mapping option (paper or digital), Google Docs, and so on. Often people argue that students can still participate in the paper-based activity by orally answering and having someone write the answers. Although this is expedient, it often relegates those same students to the role of helper and leaves them dependent on others to demonstrate their understanding or ideas. If the goal is learner agency, by varying the methods, you recognize variability and enable everyone to actively participate. At the same time you challenge all students to use different methods for brainstorming, widening everyone's perception of the ways to communicate, think, and learn.

At the Wade In level when you use different tools, it is also important to talk about these different methods with learners. Make your reasons for including them explicit, and highlight their effectiveness. This not only shows you value these alternatives, but it also helps learners become meta-cognizant of the best ways for them to organize and express ideas.

> ***Tweet:*** Varying the methods and materials used to capture ideas supports variability and enables everyone to actively participate. At the same time, it challenges all students to use different methods, widening everyone's perception of the ways to communicate, think, and learn. #DiveIntoUDL

Optional Activity

At the bottom of the Biomes lesson page is an optional activity in which students are asked to write a description of an imaginary plant or animal and its adaptations.

This is a good example of the goal and means being connected. Asking students to demonstrate their knowledge in different ways is definitely an option. If you wanted learners to practice descriptive or expository writing, however, you would need to provide a variety of technology tools and options to support completion. This might include concept mapping software, digital and paper graphic organizers to plan, video and audio options to record ideas or the entire description, and speech-to-text and word-prediction tools.

Next Steps

As you read our suggestions for ways to implement UDL in the Biomes lesson, you may have thought of different activities, materials, or tools. Terrific! The goal was to provide you with an example and ideas, not step-by-step instructions. How you implement the lesson (or your own lesson) is up to you.

However, you may be asking, what do I do next after I teach the UDL version of this lesson? You may want to:

- Discuss what happened in your lesson with colleagues (if you are working with them, and we hope you are). If they taught the same lesson, talk about what worked, where you still have questions, what you might do next.

- Repeat the experience and apply the same strategies in another lesson. Perhaps you want to make sure you share your thinking with the students so they too understand the reasons for the changes you are making.

- Continue to focus on the same areas—Instructional Goals, Accessible Materials, Resources and Tools, and Agency— building them out by exploring other aspects at the Wade In level and/or moving on to the Shallow Swim.

Website Activities

- Explore other areas of the UDL Planning Guide, staying at your current Wade In level as you build your understanding across the three domain categories.

Remember, you can access the UDL Planning Guide and more on the book's companion site by scanning the QR code.

Shallow Swim: Building Skills, Taking Ownership

At the Shallow Swim level, which focuses on the Build layer of the UDL Guidelines, you'll begin to share ownership of learning with your students. Although you'll continue to design and direct most of the learning, the experience is a shared one in which students have more options and choice, including how, and with which tools, they'll use to demonstrate their learning. At this stage, the teacher ensures learners can access a variety of technology tools (that are accessible to a wide range of students) to creatively share their deepening understanding. Rather than "cover" the curriculum, the teacher takes time to go deeper. Students are given hands-on, experiential opportunities to build conceptual understanding, as well as guided planning and strategy development to build strategies for learning. Students also build out their personal goal setting, creating more detailed plans based on their growing understanding of their learning needs. The teacher continues to "think aloud" focusing on executive functions and self-regulation skills, making them visible to the learner, and giving them opportunities to discuss and try out these skills in a safe classroom community.

Figure 9.1 Rather than provide ready-made choices, at the Shallow Swim level of implementing UDL, the teacher provides a variety of recipes for students to follow and customize.

In terms of the hamburger analogy from Chapter 7, rather than have students choose from a variety of burgers, the teacher provides a variety of recipes (Figure 9.1). The recipes allow everyone to create their own burgers, with guidance. The skill of burger making is perfected, while allowing for customization for those who prefer to add their own flair. This guided process ensures that burger making is explicit and helps learners experiment, apply strategies, and learn which techniques work best for them. Over time, and with hands-on opportunities, learners gradually assume responsibility for making their own burger.

Back to the Biomes Lesson

At the Shallow Swim level, you have a variety of ways to give learners more ownership of their learning, while ensuring they have the strategies, skills, and reflective practices they need to be successful. There are many aspects of the PBS LearningMedia Biomes lesson that we could alter, but, again, our goal is to take an iterative approach: to narrow our focus and deepen our exploration, rather than go wide and shallow. In this example we will use the UDL Planning Guide to focus on:

- **Flexible Instructional Design Category:** Physical Environment and Social Environment
- **Deep Inquiry and Understanding Category**: Authentic Learning Opportunities and Knowledge Curation and Construction

Physical Environment

The topic of habitats and biomes is an excellent starting point for ongoing discussions about the classroom environment. As you explore stresses on environments and their effects on the vegetation and animal life, there are many connections to the classroom. Recognizing that different animals rely on the physical environment in a variety of ways, and that the environment has to be flexible to meet each animal's needs, provides an excellent opportunity for you and the students to explore ways to create a more flexible classroom environment that works for everyone.

We focused on Physical Environment under the Flexible Instructional Design category. (Remember, you can access the pages of the UDL Planning Guide via the QR code at the end of Chapter 7.)

Classroom Design Inspirations

Before working with your students, review the two excellent resources available via the QR code at the end of the chapter. The first is the 360 UDL Classroom (**bit.ly/DiveIntoUDLCh8a**). This interactive tool will give you a variety of ideas to support your varied learners and give them independence to make choices within their learning environment. The second is a short video called "Classroom of the Future at Chimo Elementary" (**bit.ly/DiveIntoUDLCh8b**), which showcases the design and instructional changes seventh- and eighth-grade teacher Jennifer Strickland and her class implemented (Figure 9.2). It will give you a plethora of ideas to help you build in active ways for students to take ownership of their learning. You may not have access to all the many technology options shown in the video, but some of the low-tech ideas, such as the variety of whiteboard surfaces are doable in most classrooms. Beyond the tools, what struck us was the learner expertise of the students, working purposefully and collaboratively, within an unstructured, yet focused environment. *This* is UDL in action.

Figure 9.2 Collaboration, choice, freedom of movement, and a variety of tools, both analog and digital, are hallmarks of the "Classroom of the Future at Chimo Elementary."

To redesign your classroom into a more flexible learning environment, you could:

- Create centers with access to tools, resources, and support to complete tasks or build necessary skills to complete tasks.
- Create a tactile area that provides tools for creating, planning, modeling, and building concepts—including math manipulatives, art supplies, plasticine, building materials, and so on.
- Have students reflect on their choices and use of different classroom seating options, as well as the impact of these choices on their learning/executive functions.
- Seek student input for classroom design and use.

If you haven't created centers for your classroom before, the Biomes lesson is a good opportunity to do so. Centers are not only for students in the early grades. They are an excellent way to gradually release responsibility for learning to students of all ages, because they allow for freedom of choice within a structured setting. In the Biomes lesson centers can be set up to accommodate the various types of resources the students will explore, the materials they may need, or the technology they will use to help them answer the essential questions on the topic. This might include print resources, computer or iPad stations, materials for building or creating, and a listening/viewing center. To build in even more choice and independence into the design and use of the centers, have students work with you to determine the routines and rules for use.

At the Shallow Swim level, we assume your classroom is not organized in rows (unless you are in a shared space). You may already have students sitting in groups (with their desks facing each other). Or, you may have some flexible seating options around the classroom and you would like to further redefine the space. Although you can make changes to the room on your own, consider involving students, giving them some voice and choice in where they work and how they move about the classroom.

To set the stage, ask your students to imagine their classroom as a biome. Rather than a place for food and shelter, their biome needs to be designed to help them focus, feel comfortable, and support the different ways they learn. Then show them a picture of a very traditional classroom, such as Figure 9.3.

Share out what problems they see in the classroom design. Tell students you want their help creating a better classroom biome. To help spark ideas, you may also want to share with them the 360 UDL Classroom example (see the sidebar "Classroom Design Inspirations"). Depending on their understanding of executive function and their learning needs, do a "thumbs up/thumbs down" activity as you examine the different areas of the class and read the accompanying popups. Ask questions such as: Would this area or design support your

Figure 9.3 The traditional classroom environment is a very structured, but not necessarily effective, biome.

learning, focus, planning, motivation, and so on? Would you be able to use this area and its tools independently, or would you need support? Then, have students turn to a partner to discuss their reasons for the thumbs up or down, as well as alternatives or additions that might better support them as learners. Point out technology options that include "assistive technologies" to ensure they are recognized as an important part of the design (UDL Guidelines: Options for perception and physical action). In a class discussion, create a list of suggestions or draw a classroom map outlining changes. Or, consider having students design their ideal classrooms (biomes) by drawing, writing, or recording their ideas with an explanation of how the changes would support them. Some examples are a relaxation corner to go to when they feel anxious, stressed, or in need of a quiet place to read; the option to stand (and move freely) to help them focus as they record their ideas on a large whiteboard or table; and the option of headsets to block sound or listen to music to help with concentration while they work.

Regardless of how the ideas are collected and shared, implement some of the suggestions. Through observation and student reflection, observe the impact on learners, the effect on classroom routines or rules, and their value to support the UDL principles of Engagement, Representation, or Action and Expression, before determining whether to make the change a permanent part of the classroom environment.

Social Environment

Once again, both the topic and the group activities in this revised Biomes lesson lend themselves to building community and collaboration within your classroom. Biomes and the interconnectedness of species is a perfect opportunity to explore how actions within the class "biome" can support or interfere with others.

We focused on Social Environment under the Flexible Instructional Design category. Once again, at the Shallow Swim level, we chose three areas for the Biomes lesson:

- Have students help design processes, procedures, and class routines.
- Lead collaborative teams through a project process—setting goals, determining roles, meeting responsibilities, and so on. Deconstruct the experience and establish protocols for group work.
- Promote positive peer feedback including suggestions for improvement.

Class Routines

When students understand how the species in a biome "work together," revisit a class procedure or routine. Examine whether it is working for everyone and what changes might improve the process or routine for everyone. For example, rather than have one morning activity written on the board for students to follow, provide two or three options with the goal of completing one before the morning announcements and the day begins. Some activities may be more social, others quieter to address the variability of how learners start their morning (UDL Guidelines: Options for recruiting interest). Students could also provide input into the type and purpose of the activities in the morning routine.

Another interesting "routine" to explore with your students is the level of noise in the classroom for various activities. Often it is the teacher determining the level and enforcing the volume. Again, bring students into the discussion and decision-making process. Throughout the day, stop the class to examine the current classroom volume. Together, determine the range of acceptable noise level based on the activity, the required social interactions as well as personal preferences. As you work with students to establish acceptable noise ranges, and their enforcement of them, it is an excellent opportunity to discuss variability (for noise tolerance) and the need to ensure everyone in the class has an environment that supports their needs (UDL Guidelines: Options for recruiting interest, sustaining effort and persistence, and self-regulation).

Collaborative Group Work

As teams begin their biome research projects, take the opportunity to establish and highlight the process of successful research teams. As a class, use, edit, or create a project rubric to guide collaborative tasks and help define roles and responsibility. Throughout the short project, bring teams together to discuss how they are working as a team and provide feedback to groups and individuals based on the rubric.

The rubric might include engagement with the task, responsibility for parts of the assignment, flexibility taking on various team roles, problem solving, planning and execution, deadlines and commitments, and so on (UDL Guideline: Options for executive function, Options for effort and persistence, and self-regulation). In addition, consider using the rubric to introduce or refine peer feedback. Teach students to provide constructive criticism by offering a positive, as well as a suggestion for improvement.

When the project is complete, have teams review the rubric, make suggestions to improve it, and create guidelines for teams in the future. This resource could then be used by individuals and teams for future projects.

The sample rubrics, such as the Collaboration Rubric, provided by the Buck Institute for Education (**www.bie.org**) and included on the book's companion website (**bit.ly/DiveIntoUDLCh8c** and **bit.ly/DiveIntoUDLCh8d**), could also be used for peer feedback. This type of feedback requires trust, respect, and commitment to the process. Keep feedback observational and positive when students first begin. As students gain understanding of variability and appreciate the strengths each peer brings, expand feedback to include suggestions for improvement. Your feedback could mirror this process with "two glows and a grow" for younger students or "sandwich feedback"—positive, suggestion, positive—for older students. When students are inexperienced providing peer feedback for collaborative teamwork, keep the teams small: triads or partners. This prevents the team from ostracizing or focusing on the "faults" of one team member. Lead students through this process in a very deliberate way, using the rubric as a guide. Encourage the person who received the feedback to respond, acknowledging the suggestion and offering thoughts on how they could improve. Alternately, students could personally reflect on the process after their partner has provided both a positive and a "growth" suggestion.

If you don't believe your class is ready for this type of peer feedback, use a similar process in the next section when students are assessing their work on the biome project. Focusing on how to improve research may be less intimidating than talking about behavior and team skills (UDL Guidelines: Options for executive functions and self-regulation).

Authentic Learning Opportunities

The topic of biomes can be somewhat abstract and removed. Giving students (when possible) real-life experiences and hands-on opportunities to explore local habitats brings the issues impacting the biomes closer to home. The problems aren't just ideas in a textbook or on a website anymore. If you are unable to provide hands-on experience in a real environment, consider creating some using terrariums (desert, rainforest) or build digital ones using tools such as Minecraft (**minecraft.net**).

We focused on the Authentic Learning Opportunities area under the Deep Inquiry and Understanding category. At the Shallow Swim level, we chose the following five areas for the Biomes lesson:

- Provide students experiential learning opportunities to actively engage in first-hand documentation and research.
- Use games and simulations in challenging ways, encouraging problem solving and experimentation.

- Guide students through problem-solving activities to establish strategies and methods.
- Rather than assign topics, provide students with options to explore within an area of the curriculum.
- When possible, provide students with real-life problems, within their community and beyond, to explore and solve.

Lesson Introduction

In the Biomes lesson, there is little focus on recruiting student interest. Why should the students care about biomes? How are they relevant to their lives? How could students experience and explore biomes without completing a worksheet?

The goal is for students to understand the components of a biome, how the animals and plants within that biome are interdependent, and the impact humans (and other natural occurrences) have on biomes. (For a reminder of how to separate the goals and the means to demonstrate the learning, review Chapter 8.)

Begin by sharing with students that the natural habitat around their school is under stress. It is their job is to understand the surrounding habitat, how it functions, and what is threatening it. You may want to use recent events, both natural and human made, to determine some possible threats to the habitats in your area (UDL Guideline: Options for recruiting interest).

If possible, begin by introducing students to a habitat they can personally experience via a walking tour or class field trip. Even the schoolyard will suffice. Tell students their goal is to define what a habitat is, consider how the elements (plants and animals) work together, and what, if any, evidence there is of changes that might impact the habitat. They can document evidence by taking pictures, sketching, or recording observations of the various components they think define a habitat. Depending on the age of your students or their experience documenting evidence, discuss how they might organize themselves as they complete this task. Highlight that the goal is to define the word "habitat," not just list things *in* the habitat.

For some students, you may want to include a mini-teach, exploring a visual habitat book with them to discuss the headings they notice, to act as a guide as they complete the activity.

If your students are unable to physically experience a habitat, have them watch a video and capture pictures, sketch, or record their observations in a similar manner. This might work ever better as a center, where students screen capture and document directly into a folder, portfolio, or even Google Slides. For older students who have already explored habitats in a lower grade, you may want to move directly to the exploration of biomes and the biome game (page 147).

Once students have explored their physical or virtual habitat, come together to talk about their discoveries. Together, using their field notes, discuss the vegetation, animals, weather, and other elements of this local area. This information could be collected in a Google Doc or using an online tool such as SMART Notebook Express (**express.smarttech.com**). Once the habitat is defined, pair and then square students to discuss the various threats or stress they recorded. Come together again as a class to record the various threats and, if desired, order them in terms of severity or negative impact on the environment or sort them according to natural versus human cause. Explain that the habitat they explored is part of a larger biome, a community of living things that often adapt to the various conditions (climate, soil, etc.) in that area. Using a site such as the Missouri Botanical Garden's Biomes of the World site (**www.mbgnet.net**), have students identify where their local habitat fits, and then work together to create a definition for biomes including keywords: climate, environmental factors, plants, animals, and so on. Tell students they will use this definition to help with their research later.

Biome Game

To assess learners' readiness and continue to build understanding, play a biome game. Provide options for answering, such as voting apps, clickers, drawing programs on iPads, individual whiteboards, or notepaper. If possible, create a digital version of the biome. This could be created in an online program such as Habitat Maker (**mrnussbaum.com/habitatmaker2**) or within Google Slides using images from Pixabay (**pixabay.com**) or other creative commons licensed images. Create several slides that introduce or remove various animals and plants, change the climate or environmental conditions, or add an event (storm, human interaction). Then have students indicate the impact on the biome using their voting method. This could be a rating scale or a set of adjectives to describe the impact.

Follow up with a class discussion to review how the elements of the biome are balanced, and how human and natural changes impact species and, sometimes, entire biomes.

Knowledge Curation and Construction

Take a look at the Knowledge Curation and Construction focus under the Deep Inquiry and Understanding category. At the Shallow Swim level, we chose the following four areas to implement for the Biomes lesson:

- Provide multiple entry points to a lesson and optional pathways through content (for example, exploring big ideas through dramatic works, arts and literature, film and media).
- Provide students with templates and guides to help them plan and use effective research strategies to locate information and other resources for their intellectual or creative pursuits.
- Provide students with various tools and outline various methods students can use to curate information from digital resources to create collections of artifacts that demonstrate meaningful connections or conclusions.

- With a variety of templates and frameworks available, have students ask questions and design projects to actively explore real-world issues and solve authentic problems.

Research

Once students understand the basic concepts related to habitats and biomes, create triads to complete a jigsaw activity. Limiting the number of students in the group will support the Social Environment focus mentioned earlier, because group members will have fewer personalities to contend with as they critically examine their roles in making collaborative groups function successfully. Assign each triad a biome. For learners who may still need extra practice, assign them the class biome already reviewed.

Tell students that similar problems to those they encountered in their local biome are happening worldwide. Their goal is to work with their group to better understand a particular biome, determine any threats to it, and then come together as a class to determine any trends and possible strategies to minimize or remove the threats. Next, post the class-curated biome definition and keywords created earlier, and together create a graphic organizer to help collect information. The graphic organizer could be first sketched on chart paper, and then when the class agrees on the design, created online in Google Docs or using a free graphic design tool, such as Canva (**https://www.canva.com/create/graphic-organizers**). Model using the organizer in both a paper and digital environment, and ask for suggestions for alternate ways the students might choose to collect the information, such as using digital folders, note-taking, or concept maps (UDL Guidelines: Options for comprehension).

As a team, students will research their biome to gather the required information, including what activity or changes are negatively impacting it. The goal of the team is for each member to understand the elements of the biome and the dangers it faces. And each member should have a method to collect and share his or her information with others. When students are finished, create cross-biome teams of seven. This will require more structure and rules than the triads needed. As such, you may need to discuss, role-play, and model various roles, turn taking, and decision-making within a large group.

Then ask the students: What is endangering biomes, what are the world-wide trends, and what should we do about it? Each member of the team will briefly share information on their biome and the dangers it faces. (Depending on time, you may ask students to create a simple presentation, one-page overview, or short video to accompany their information. The key is for them to consider accessibility of their resource, making sure everyone can access it.) Other members can ask questions, and one member will record the concerns and dangers. When finished, the team works together to answer the first part of the question to determine if there are any similarities and trends. They can also discuss possible solutions.

After sharing each cross-biome team's findings, work as a class to summarize the information. This data might be shared on a large map of the world or documented in a spreadsheet. Once possible solutions have been shared and discussed, bring the triads back together. Their job is to choose one or two solutions to support their biome, verify the validity of the suggestions, and then determine how to share their findings with others. This might include Public Service Announcements (PSAs), teaching younger students, blogging, or creating videos.

Next Steps

As you read our suggestions to implement UDL in the Biomes lesson at the Shallow Swim level, you may have thought of different activities, materials, or tools. Terrific! The goal was to provide you with an example and ideas, not step-by-step instructions. How you implement the lesson (or your own lesson) is up to you.

However, you may be asking, what do I do next after I teach this UDL version of this lesson? Here are our suggestions. You may want to:

- Discuss what happened in your lesson with colleagues (if you are working with them, and we hope you are). If they taught the same lesson, talk about what worked, where you still have questions, what you might do next.

- Repeat the experience and apply the same strategies in another lesson. Perhaps you want to make sure you share your thinking with the students so they, too, understand the reasons for the changes you are making.

- Continue to focus on the same areas, building them out by exploring other aspects at the Shallow Swim level and/or moving on to the Deep Dive.

- Deeply explore all three areas of the UDL Planning Guide, staying at your current Shallow Swim level as you build your understanding across the three categories.

Website Activities

Remember, you can access the UDL Planning Guide and more on the book's companion site by scanning the QR code.

Deep Dive: Internalizing Skills, Building Learner Expertise

At the Deep Dive level of UDL implementation, your students take ownership of their learning as you subtly guide and direct the learning to best support their growing independence, as embodied in the Internalize layer of the UDL Guidelines. At this stage, the teacher continues to introduce key concepts and support learners with small group mini-teaches, centers, and teacher-created support videos, the students often determine what they will learn and how they will learn it. They understand themselves as learners, know what technology best supports and enhances their learning, as well as what technology best represents their learning. They can effectively set goals, plan, implement, and assess their own learning with greater and growing awareness and skill, focused on growth over time.

To summarize this level using our hamburger analogy: Rather than creating a burger from a variety of recipes, everyone is allowed to design their own burger from a wide array of choices. They know the tools and the ingredients, as well as their skills and abilities. Experimentation and personal preference are encouraged (Figure 10.1). Some may choose to continue to use a recipe to build their burger. Others may create a "burger fit for a gourmet food truck." Some may use the ingredients to make a salad.

Figure 10.1. At the Deep Dive level of UDL implementation, learners possess the skills and experience to independently design and create their own learning from an array of ingredients.

The goal at this level is to move away from teacher-directed and -owned instruction, but it doesn't have to happen all at once. There are many factors, such as district requirements, student readiness, and professional preference that will determine how this type of learning is implemented. Some approaches that can help you move from less to more student-driven learning are:

- **Per Term/Unit**: After a unit or term study, students complete short inquiry-based or cross-curricular (STEAM) projects. The topic is often established by the teacher (with many of the skills and concepts studied during the unit), while the learner creates the question(s), plans the project, and determines the final product for sharing. Unlike the previous Shallow Swim projects, for which the educator provides more direct guidance and modeling then works with the learners to develop graphic organizers and rubrics, for this Deep Dive project learners have many of the collaborative, planning, and technology skills to independently complete the projects.

- **Percent/Portion of Week**: Each week students are given set periods of time (20% Club, Genius Hour) to explore ideas, questions, or subjects deeply. The teacher guides the process, helping them refine their questions and determine required prerequisite skills before providing scaffolds, resources, adaptive instruction, or direct instruction to build these skills.

- **Whole Units** or **Entire Program**: Project-based learning (PBL) is a shift to a very different approach to learning. In PBL, teachers plan the driving question, the introductory event, scaffolding or support activities, timeline (for completion), assessment rubrics, and the culminating event. Students can be invited in to help co-plan any of the above items. They then determine the rest, including the exploration of other, unplanned questions or directions (with reason and purpose).

Back to the Biomes Lesson

By the time you reach the Deep Dive level of implementing UDL, students already have many of the skills needed to be expert learners. They have experience setting goals, using rubrics for assessment, planning and organizing their work, and better understanding themselves as learners. You still, however, need to plan for variability even at this stage, recognizing that some students will continue to need teacher support and guidance to plan, make good decisions, and understand their learning needs. There are many aspects of the Biomes lesson that we could alter, but, again, our goal is to take an iterative approach: to narrow our focus and deepen our exploration, rather than go wide and shallow. In this example, we will use the UDL Planning Guide and focus on areas in all three domains:

- **Flexible Instructional Design Category:** Formative Assessment and Feedback
- **Deep Inquiry and Understanding Category:** Authentic Learning Opportunities and Open Creation and Communication
- **Ownership of Learning Category:** Reflection and Metacognition and Executive Function

Formative Assessment and Feedback, and Reflection and Metacognition

Assessment is often viewed as evaluation, a summative task in a written form. If our goal is learner expertise and ownership of learning, students need ongoing opportunities to assess the process (and not just the product) of learning. At the reflection level, they gain understanding of what they learned. At the metacognitive level, they gain understanding of how they think and the strategies that help them learn.

In this section we combined two categories, as they are interconnected. Take a look at the Formative Assessment and Feedback focus under the Flexible Instructional Design category, as well as the Reflection and Metacognition focus under the Ownership of Learning category. (Remember, you can access pages of the UDL Planning Guide via the QR code at the end of Chapter 7.) At the Deep Dive level, we chose several areas to concentrate on for our makeover of the PBS LearningMedia Biomes lesson:

Formative Assessment and Feedback

- Have students co-design their own success criteria: rubrics, checklists, and so on, to be used for feedback and formative assessment.
- Expand timely, usable feedback—written and verbal—across curriculum areas with a continued focus on growth and acceptance of mistakes as part of learning.
- Create a formative assessment loop within a digital portfolio to include teacher feedback, student reflection and next steps, and parent comments and advice.

Self-Reflection and Metacognition

- Have students verbalize/record how they learn best, the strategies they use, and their next steps for improvement.
- Encourage student self-reflection before, during, and after completion of tasks, focusing on growth, a "not yet" mindset, and a willingness to learn from their mistakes.

The original Biomes lesson is a typical teacher-directed lesson with a summative assessment at the end. There is some discussion but little ongoing formative assessment or student reflection.

The goal of assessment is to guide learning, focusing less on assessment *of* learning (achievement) and more on assessment *for* learning (progress) and assessment *as* learning (growth). Rather than waiting until the end of a lesson or unit and then opting to test, quiz, or mark an end product, assessment for learning (AfL) is an ongoing process. AfL helps you determine where your students are in their learning, where they need to go next, and the actionable steps to get there. Assessment as learning encourages students to actively assess themselves, rather than be passive recipients of grades. Again, this is an ongoing activity in which the learner focuses on what is going well and why, as well as what needs to improve and how. Guiding students through this process goes a long way to helping them purposefully direct and own their learning.

Using our swim analogy, assessment *for* learning is the coaching that happens while the swimmer is in the water. The coach encourages the swimmer, helps him correct or improve his stroke, oversee his practice attempts. Assessment *as* learning is the swimmer analyzing herself. She may watch a video of her performance or repeatedly practice her turn around until it feels right. Assessment *of* learning is the swimmer's placement in the final race.

Learning Portfolios/Reflection

One way to support the various forms of assessment is through the use of ePortfolios. Rather than create "showcase" portfolios of finished products to be evaluated, students document their learning over time by saving artifacts related to each stage of their biome inquiry. Use the portfolio to encourage two-way "for and as" conversations. You can leave mastery-oriented feedback for learners that includes questions, next steps, and a simple mastery scale (1–4) if desired. This evidence of student learning can also inform your next steps: the strategies, scaffolding, and resources students need to help them move forward in the project (UDL Guideline: Options for sustaining effort and persistence).

The ePortfolios support ownership of learning as students gather and curate evidence of their learning using video, images, audio, uploads, links, and text (UDL Guideline: Options for expression and communication). Students use the portfolio to record their thoughts about the project, its processes, products, and next steps, as well as respond to teacher feedback, suggestions, and questions. To encourage metacognition, ask students to pause before, during, and after a task to "think about their thinking." This helps students become more aware of their thought processes and how they can direct them to improve their learning. Although students could keep a separate journal, having them record in their ePortfolios allows them to review their evidence of learning and helps integrate metacognitive reflections within the iterative design process. As you ask or suggest questions, ensure learners focus on *how* they learned rather than *what* they learned. Here are some sample questions for metacognition students could ask themselves at various stages of the project:

1. **Before a task:** What is my goal for this task? What strengths or skills do I bring to this task? What about the task might be difficult for me? Are there any technology tools to help me? Do I know what is expected of me? Can I see the big picture? Can I break the task into manageable steps?

2. **During the task:** Does what I'm doing make sense to me? Am I focused or distracted? Am I organized? Am I meeting my goals and deadlines? What should I keep doing? What should I change? What tools, resources, or people might help me?

3. **After a task:** What strategies worked well? Which tools and resources helped me complete the task? What could I do differently or better? Does the finished product represent my skills and knowledge? What takeaways can I apply to the next task?

A portfolio could be as simple as a folder on Google Drive or in Microsoft OneNote (**onenote.com**), or students could create one in a portfolio app, such as SeeSaw (**web.seesaw.me**) or FreshGrade (**freshgrade.com**) (UDL Guideline: Options for self-regulation).

Rubrics

Another tool to support assessment, feedback, and reflection that students can upload and reference in their portfolio is a rubric. Rather than assign students a project rubric, start with one you designed, and then guide students through the process of customizing it. This gives them an opportunity to shape the criteria for success and helps to ensure they have a voice in how they are assessed.

Avoid rubrics that act as to-do lists—include three pictures, include five references—as they do not fit well with project-based learning or other student-directed activities. Rubrics should focus on processes and transferable skills across projects, rather than act as a project checklist or requirements for completion (UDL Guidelines: Options for sustaining effort and persistence).

Authentic Learning Opportunities

Allowing learners to make decisions around the questions they will ask and ultimately what they will learn can be a challenge in the current education system with standardized testing and accountability. These types of learning experiences, however, do not need to be all or nothing. Giving students authentic learning opportunities in which they (almost) completely drive the process is possible on a smaller scale.

Take a look at the Authentic Learning Opportunities focus under the Deep Inquiry and Understanding category. At the Deep Dive level, we chose the following to concentrate on for the Biomes lesson:

- Give students opportunities to connect and collaborate with others from around the world on authentic, real-world problems that involve data collection, solution generation, and so on.
- Provide students with opportunities and time to explore topics of personal interest or concern.

The Biomes lesson is one that can't help calling to mind author David Loertscher's advice to "Ban the bird unit!" As Loertscher (Loertscher, Koechlin, and Zwaan, 2005) described, a "bird unit," named after the ubiquitous fourth-grade bird report, is a low-level task in which the student records what the bird eats, where the bird lives, what the bird looks like ... you get the idea. Jamie McKenzie, editor of *From Now On: The Educational Technology Journal*, calls this type of inquiry a "go find out about" lesson, for which students easily copy and paste information into a report, rather than sort and sift through information to answer a question or solve a problem.

To avoid the "bird unit" aspects of this lesson, you will explore features of project-based learning (PBL) and their application to this lesson. Rather than sending them off to learn about biomes, present students with a challenge related to environmental change. They could investigate problems affecting their community or explore problems on a global scale. To facilitate this, consider platforms such as iEARN (**https://iearn.org**) or Taking IT Global (**https://www.tigweb.org**) where students have opportunities to collaborate on purposeful global projects. This helps ensure the learning is authentic by relating the key concepts of the lesson to real-life problems impacting real people, whether in their community or around the world. Local examples might be the long-term impact of the BP oil spill on the plants and animals of the Florida Gulf Coast where Luis lives. Or, the environmental and economic impact caused by the introduction of zebra mussels into the Great Lakes where Kendra lives. A global example could be studying the impact of human behavior on river health with others in several countries around the world (UDL Guidelines: Options for recruiting interest).

PBL is similar to UDL in that it takes time to implement. Many aspects of the skills students need to be successful within a PBL unit are similar to those of an expert learner. In this chapter, we will only touch briefly on PBL, in particular the driving question or scenario that sets the stage for learners.

While wading in during Chapter 8, we separated the lesson goals from the means and created more specific, measurable goals stated in student-friendly language. As you may remember, they were:

At the end of this lesson, I will be able to:

- Identify my biome type (terrestrial or aquatic) and include three (3) reasons for my identification.
- Describe at least three (3) environmental factors and five (5) native plants and animals of my biome.
- Show my understanding of how environmental factors are interdependent with the plants and animals within my biome.
- Identify at least three (3) similarities and three (3) differences between my own biome and a partner's biome.
- Describe at least three (3) examples of plant and animal adaptations found in my biome.

To better address the intent of the PBL aspects of this lesson, we will add three additional goals:

- Explain, with carefully cited evidence, the cause(s) and impact of biome change.

- Outline possible solutions or supports to address, remove, or lessen the impact on a particular biome.
- Recognize the impact trends, and related solutions, to summarize global changes and actions.

Driving Question or Scenario

One way to present a challenge or problem for study is to create a scenario similar to the one below. You would then present, playing the role of Dr. Smith. While the character might be imaginary, the information and urgency would be real:

> Hello, I am Dr. Smith. I am the head of PBE—Protect Biomes Everywhere. Recently, a number of incidents around the world have severely impacted the wildlife, vegetation, and the livelihood of the residents in these areas. We are looking for a team to first assess the environmental changes these event have caused, and to provide us with suggestions to mitigate the damage, protect the biome from further damage, and if possible, prevent something similar from happening in the future. In three weeks you will need to report to our committee.

This role-play approach avoids the "teacher questions" after the fact. Once Dr. Smith is gone, the teacher can't answer any questions the doctor might know, or re-explain what the doctor shared. Over time students learn to develop and ask clarifying questions, shifting their problem-solving skills away from the teacher as solution provider. This can be a frustrating experience for some students, but it will help them grow as independent learners.

Open Creation and Communication

Being effective communicators and creators is no longer dependent on limited methods (writing) or complex technology tools. This opens the door for all learners (UDL Guidelines: Options for communication and expression). When working with creative tools, teachers have the opportunity to emphasize the importance of accessibility and how design can interfere with audience understanding. This reinforces the message of UDL. By the time you reach the Deep Dive implementation level of UDL, your students should, with limited support, be able to identify the medium and message that addresses both the intent of the activity, as well as the learning needs of the creator and the audience.

We focused on Open Creation and Communication under the Deep Inquiry and Understanding category. (Remember, you can access the pages of the UDL Planning Guide via the QR code at the end of Chapter 7.) At the Deep Dive level, we chose the following areas to concentrate on for the Biomes lesson:

- Students understand and independently select the appropriate platforms and tools to support the completion of the task and meet the objectives of their creation or communication.

- Students use an iterative approach, garnering feedback to improve their message and product, before sharing with the intended audience.

- Give students authentic opportunities to publish or present content that customizes the message and medium for their intended audiences.

Project Activities

After students are introduced to the challenge, problem, or scenario, tell them they need to organize their team. This might include setting up their portfolios, setting team goals and deadlines, and exploring the various rubrics to guide their research and group work. If portfolios are new to students, provide guidance as they upload their plans and assessment rubrics to their portfolios. Once this is done, their second task is to plan their basic research on their biome. Students should have experience with research, but always ensure various scaffolds are available for those who still need them, including support videos, project and research planners, graphic organizers, and so on. In this project, students are still guided in their choice of media; however, you could also provide them with free choice. In their portfolios, encourage students to reflect on their choices, how they work for both the message and the audience needs.

In groups, students will create a *visual representation* of their biome from the past (mural, poster, sculpture, drawing) and a *digital presentation* of its present condition (video, image, website, audio). When complete, students take a gallery walk to learn about the other biomes to get a sense of the problems each face (UDL Guidelines: Options for expression and communication). This would also be a good opportunity for peer feedback in which students make suggestions to improve the message or the media.

After teams have learned about the various biomes and the problems they face, groups then focus on finding solutions for their biome. They can choose any method of presentation to demonstrate the various solutions to the PBE. This might include creating a model such as the beach, a desert, or rainforest in a terrarium, an online environment in Minecraft (**minecraft.net**), a biome created with an online tool such as Habitat Maker (**mrnussbaum.com/habitatmaker2**), or a video using a green screen. This is an excellent opportunity to talk about accessibility as students create their solutions, engaging in conversations about the barriers their methods present and ways to ensure more people can interact with and learn from their presentation.

You may want to include a follow-up written report from each student as would often be requested if presenting an idea to a committee. Because this lesson is at the Deep Dive level, students will automatically have access to and understand the best use of various tools and resources to help them complete the task. This would include paper and digital writing frameworks, graphic organizers for planning, access to speech-to-text tools, apps such as PaperPort Notes (Nuance Communications, **paperportnotes.com**), and word-prediction tools such as WordQ (Quillsoft Ltd., **goqsoftware.com/wordQ.php**), or Read&Write for Google Chrome (Texthelp Ltd., **texthelp.com**) (UDL Guidelines: Options for perception and physical action). Focusing the task on summarizing important issues, identifying worldwide trends, and categorizing solutions would elevate the activity to include higher-order thinking (UDL Guidelines: Options for comprehension).

Executive Function

Executive function, intersecting with self-regulation, acts as a conductor, orchestrating mental processes and emotions that help students navigate learning and social situations. The importance of these mental processes is emphasized within the UDL principles, appearing as key guidelines in the development of learner expertise (UDL Guidelines: Options for self-regulation, Options for executive function). These important skills are, however, often associated with classroom management, behaviors to be controlled by the teacher, rather than self-management tools for the learner. This "hidden" curriculum is essential to student success but often left to chance. As such, many students are unaware of the effect poor executive functions have on their learning and relationships. And they often don't recognize there are actionable steps for them to take, as well as a variety of tool and strategies to help them develop and manage their executive function. Once you reach the Deep Dive level of UDL implementation, students are expected to be familiar with the term *executive functions*, having had opportunities to learn more about them and improve them. Given the importance of executive function and its ongoing development through the teen years and beyond, however, it is important to continue to emphasize and highlight aspects of it on a daily basis.

We focused on the Executive Function area under the Ownership of Learning category. At the Deep Dive level, we chose three elements to concentrate on for the Biomes lesson:

- Embed executive function into success criteria, rubrics, and assessment discussions.
- Encourage students to choose templates, checklists, strategies, online planners, and other technology tools that best support their executive functions.
- Working with students, have them build in references to executive functions within assessment rubrics and project planning.

Developing and refining executive functions is a lifelong pursuit. Indeed many learners will struggle with some of these skills, which help learners manage time, pay attention, switch focus, organize and plan, remember details, and act with control, and require support and guidance throughout high school and beyond. For this reason, consider including a focus on executive function when learners set goals for the project. There are several places to do this. One is in the project planner, where students record the tools they will use to complete the organization, team planning, note-taking, and research portion of the project. Another place is to ask questions within student's portfolios, providing them with opportunities throughout the project to reflect on their executive functions, and the tools they have chosen to support them. Or you may decide to include a reference to executive functions in the project and/or teamwork rubric that students use to assess themselves before, during, and after the project. References to organization, planning, deadlines, commitment to task, commitment to deadlines, responsibility to team, dealing with frustration, and relationships with team members are all observable forms of executive function.

In the Biomes lesson, there are many ways to support executive function that blend well with PBL, including the creation of a common or shared calendar. However, students should also be encouraged to create their own calendar or reminder. Rather than rely on apps such as Remind (**remind.com**), where the teacher reminds the students of important due dates, encourage students to be responsible for their own time management. To organize, plan, and time-manage project-based activities, shareable online tools are an asset; however, groups should work together so that the tool they choose works for every member, especially in the area of accessibility but also preference. Emphasize that one member is not in charge of the tool, and the remainder only access for updates, but that each member is responsible for the upkeep. Tools such as Trello (**trello.com**), Evernote (**evernote.com**), OneNote, and Google Keep are effective tools for the organization, time management, and execution of the project.

Next Steps

PBL is a complex process that aligns well with UDL and our focus on an iterative Wade In, Shallow Swim, and Deep Dive process. How you gradually release responsibility for learning to learners, scaffolding, modeling, and intentional focus on the process of ownership is important. Understanding that some learners will always need more support emphasizes learner variability, but also helps keep these often-invisible skills at the forefront of student learning.

Below are our suggestions for what to do next after co-teaching this UDL version of the Biomes lesson. You may want to:

- Discuss what happened in your lesson with colleagues (if you are working with them and we hope you are). If they taught the same lesson, talk about what worked, where you still have questions, what you might do next.

- Repeat the experience, and apply the same strategies in another lesson. Perhaps you want to make sure you share your thinking with the students so they too understand the reasons for the changes you are making.

- Continue to focus on the same areas, building them out by exploring other aspects at the Deep Dive level, or perhaps moving back one level if your understanding or the student's understanding isn't yet fully developed.

- Explore other areas of the UDL Planning Guide, building out more and connecting the three categories.

Remember, you can access the UDL Planning Guide and more on the book's companion site by scanning the QR code.

Website Activities

Conclusion

One of Kendra's favorite movies is *Finding Nemo* (Stanton et al., 2003). A fish with active working memory issues "just keeps swimming," moving forward towards her goal (even when she forgets it). Ever optimistic, she believes she has the skills (to talk to whales) and the network (remember the turtles?) to help her when she needs it. Along the way, she meets a lot of variability. Each creature has something to offer and teach, even the ADHD seagulls. We hope you are just as optimistic, but perhaps not as forgetful as Dory the fish, as you explore and apply UDL principles to your practice.

UDL isn't a destination like 42 Wallaby Way. It's a journey, taken together with other professionals who are eager to learn, share, and improve their practices. Consider this book in your hands (or on your device) as both a conduit and a catalyst—a conduit to connect with us and others interested in transforming their practices, and a catalyst, the spark to help you take on the challenge of change. We mean it when we say we hope you will connect with us and make us your #UDLPeeps. You can reach Kendra at @kendrafgrant and Luis at @eyesonaxs on Twitter, and use #DiveIntoUDL to share your successes, your learning, and your questions.

Part 3 of this book has been dedicated to taking a lesson and infusing it with elements of UDL. We explored three areas using the UDL Planning Guide as a map along our journey. Flexible Instructional Design has many of the implementation elements associated with UDL implementation, but goes further to include the social and physical elements of the classroom, the third teacher. Next, we explored Deep Inquiry and Understanding, which points to the heart of UDL (learner expertise) and to the intent of the ISTE Standards (empowered learners who can drive their own learning). Finally, we explored and brought to the surface, the "hidden" curriculum: the self-awareness, habits of mind and self-regulation needed if students are to become purposeful learners, who understand as much about themselves and others as they do about traditional classroom subjects. Ultimately, the hidden curriculum may be the most important of all, improving learning, but also positively impacting well-being, mental health, and social confidence.

As you come to the end of the book, we encourage you to take some time to reflect on the progress you have made and the insights you have gained about both your learners and your own learning. Like a novice swimmer, your initial attempts at introducing UDL into your lessons may have seemed uncomfortable and required some effort. With the strategies and understanding you have gained from reading this book, you should now be developing a smoother stroke that allows you to swim further and faster than before. If you were at the Wade In level of UDL when you started the book, on your next read, challenge yourself and move up to a Shallow Swim. Or if you were already at that level, see if you can take your skills up a notch by exploring the Deep Dive sections of the book. We designed this book to allow you to take an iterative approach, returning to specific sections as your own understanding of UDL grows and you are ready to move to even higher levels of expertise in your practice as an inclusive educator.

In addition to continuing to use the book as a tool for ongoing reflection and revision of your lessons with the help of the UDL Planning Guide, we encourage you to work with other educators to expand the reach of UDL at your school and district. The changes you bring to your teaching as you adopt UDL will have even more impact if your classroom is not the only place where your learners get to experience the UDL principles and guidelines in action. There are several steps you can take to ensure UDL does not remain trapped in your classroom but spreads to other members of your community:

- **Co-teach a lesson using the UDL Planning Guide to plan, implement, and revise your lesson with a teaching partner.** This is one way to begin to expand your professional Zone of Proximal Development (see Chapter 3), focused on UDL. As you work together, your partner may bring a different perspective that you had not considered before. Just like your learners, the two of you will bring your own variability to your work. Your partner may be stronger in some areas, while you may be stronger in others. Working together, you will be able to complement each other's skills and push each other to even greater heights of teaching expertise as you bring your combined expertise to the lessons you design. World-class athletes like Michael Phelps know that working in isolation will only get them so far in their quest for high performance. They usually team up with a training partner who has similar aspirations and pushes them to break through training plateaus. In your school, is there a person who could serve as your "training partner" as you move on to the next level of UDL implementation? If not, don't worry. Connected educators from all over the world can play that role if you join an online community of practice.

- **Start a blog to document your UDL journey and share your insights with other teachers in your school and district.** A blog could serve as a learning journal that allows you to make your thinking and learning visible as you move through the various levels of UDL implementation. This would not only motivate you as you see your progress reflected over time, it would also provide helpful guidance for how to address similar learning challenges in the future. Furthermore, the blog is a great way to celebrate your successes with not only your immediate community (your school or district), but also with the broader field of education. You may find that other educators start to follow your blog and look to you for guidance and support, and you will do the same with other educators you meet through these online connections. Your blog would also be an excellent way for you to make your learning visible to your students (and parents) as you rethink your role into that of a collaborator and co-learner with them. If you decide to start a blog, we would love to feature it on the book's website. Just send us the link at **DiveIntoUDL@gmail.com**, and we'll be happy to feature it as another learning resource for our readers.

- **Join online communities of practice.** You can use the hashtag #DiveIntoUDL to connect with other readers, and there are a number of Twitter chats where educators from all over the world come together to share strategies and tools that could be helpful to you as you move forward in your UDL journey. One of our favorites is #UDLChat, a weekly chat where thought leaders and practitioners of UDL come together to share both their successes and challenges in a supportive conversation. We encourage you to participate in one of those chats, even if it is just as an observer the first few times.

As we come to the end of the book (but not the learning), we envision a huge community swimming pool, large enough for everyone. We see a variety of depths, devices, and people as we scan the pool. Some are learning to swim, and are a little fearful. Others dive in and paddle away. No one is alone, struggling. Everyone is included. We see learning in every corner of the pool, but more importantly, we see people laughing, enjoying the process, and improving every day.

Everyone who knows how to swim was once a beginner, even the great Michael Phelps. With the right support, you can make steady progress as you realize your potential and thrive. Just as water flows and escapes its container, we want UDL to flow out your classroom, seep under closed doors, and float everyone a bit higher.

We hope you'll make a big splash (share, tweet, present, blog) so that the changes you make to improve learning in your classroom —with help from this book—do not stop with you but instead have an impact on the educators, administration, curriculum, and learners at your school or district. Together, let's go forward to spread our love of learning and our passion for ensuring equity in education!

Website Activities   You can learn more on the book's companion site by scanning the QR code.

References

CAST. (2011). *Universal Design for Learning Guidelines version 2.0.* Wakefield, MA: Author.

CAST. (2017). *UDL Guidelines: UDL theory and practice version.* Retrieved from http://www.udlcenter.org/aboutudl/udlguidelines_theorypractice

CAST. (2018). UDL Guidelines. Retrieved from http://udlguidelines.cast.org

CAST. (2017). *About Universal Design for Learning.* Retrieved from http://www.cast.org

Center for Universal Design. (2008). *About UD.* Retrieved from https://projects.ncsu.edu/ncsu/design/cud/about_ud/about_ud.htm

Cole, P. (2004). Professional development: A great way to avoid change. *IARTV* (Seminar Series No. 140). Retrieved from http://www.malit.org.uk/wp-content/uploads/Peter-Cole-PD-A-great-way-to-avoid-change.pdf

Dutton, J. (May/June, 2007). They will make you proud. *ADDitude Magazine.* Retrieved from https://www.additudemag.com

Dweck, C. S. (2006). *Mindset: The new psychology of success.* New York: Random House.

Edyburn, D. (2006, September). Failure is not an option. *Leading and Learning with Technology.* Retrieved from https://erlc.wikispaces.com/file/view/Failure+is+Not+an+Option.pdf

Evmenova, A. (2008). *Lights! Camera! Captions!: The effects of picture and/or word captioning adaptations, alternative narration, and interactive features on video comprehension by students with intellectual disabilities.* Fairfax, VA: George Mason University College of Education and Human Development.

Ericsson, A., Krampe, R., & Tesch-Roemer, C. (1993). The role of deliberate practice in the acquisition of expert performance. *Psychological Review, 100* (3), 363–406.

Ford, H., & Crowther, S. (1922). *My life and work.* Garden City, New York: Garden City Publishing Company, Inc.

Fullan, M. (2007). Professional development is not professional learning. *Journal of Staff Development*. Retrieved from http://www.michaelfullan.ca

Hannay, L., Wideman, R. & Seller, W. (2006). Professional learning to reshape teaching. Elementary Teachers' Federation of Ontario in Toronto, Canada, 14.

Hirsh, S., & Killion, J. (2007). *The learning educator: A new era for professional learning*. Oxford, OH: National Staff Development Council.

Hirsh, S., Psencik, K., & Brown, F. (2014). *Becoming a learning system*. Oxford, OH: Learning Forward.

International Society for Technology in Education. (2016). *ISTE Standards for Students*. Retrieved from https://www.iste.org/standards/standards/for-students

International Society for Technology in Education. (2017). *ISTE Standards for Educators*. Retrieved from https://www.iste.org/standards/standards/for-educators

Juliani, A.J. (N.D.). *The game of school vs. the game of life*. Retrieved from http://ajjuliani.com/game-school-vs-game-life

King, A. (1993). From sage on the stage to guide on the side. *College Teaching. 41*(1), 30–35.

Krueger, N. (2017, June 24). It's like yoga for your educational practice. *ISTE Blog*. Retrieved from https://www.iste.org/explore/articleDetail?articleid=1001&category=ISTE-blog&article=

Lavoie, R. (1989). *How difficult can this be? The F.A.T city workshop* [Video file]. Eagle Hill School Outreach. Retrieved from https://www.youtube.com/watch?v=WPrDNVXt59U&feature=youtu.be

Linebarger, D. L. (2001). Learning to read from television: The effects of using captions and narration. *Journal of Educational Psychology, 93*(2), 288–298. Retrieved from http://dx.doi.org/10.1037/0022-0663.93.2.288

Loertscher, D.V., Koechlin, C., & Zwaan, S. (2005) *Ban those bird units! 15 models for teaching and learning in information-rich and technology-rich environments*. Salt Lake City, UT: Hi Willow Research and Publishing.

Meyer, A., & Rose, D. H. (2005). The future is in the margins: The role of technology and disability in educational reform. In D. H. Rose, A. Meyer & C. Hitchcock (Eds.), *The universally designed classroom: Accessible curriculum and digital technologies* (pp. 13–35). Cambridge, MA: Harvard Education Press. Retrieved from http://www.udlcenter.org/sites/udlcenter.org/files/Meyer-Rose_FutureisintheMargins.pdf

Meyer, A., Rose, D. H., & Gordon, D. (2014) *Universal design for learning: Theory and practice*. Wakefield, MA: CAST.

Ontario Ministry of Education. (2010). *Collaborative teacher inquiry*. Capacity Building Series (Secretariat Special Edition #16). Retrieved from http://www.edu.gov.on.ca/eng/literacynumeracy/inspire/research/CBS_Collaborative_Teacher_Inquiry.pdf

Owston, R. (2004). *Contextual factors that sustain innovative pedagogical practice using technology: An international study*. Paper presented at the Annual Meeting of the American Educational Research Association, San Diego, CA. Retrieved from https://pdfs.semanticscholar.org/1bff/4a9882d6f8e418e7fad31524a63496e4051e.pdf

Peters, D. (2011, October 25). Say hello to learning interface design. *UX Magazine*. Retrieved from http://uxmag.com/articles/say-hello-to-learning-interface-design

Rose, D. (2010). *UDL Guidelines structure* [Video file]. National Center on Universal Design for Learning. Retrieved from https://youtu.be/wVTm8vQRvNc

Rose, T. (2016). *The end of average: How we succeed in a world that values sameness*. San Francisco, CA, HarperOne.

Shokri, N., Lehmann, P., & Or, D. (2009), Characteristics of evaporation from partially wettable porous media, *Water Resources Research*, 45, W02415, doi:10.1029/2008WR007185

Simons, D. (2010). *Selective attention test* [Video file]. Retrieved from https://youtu.be/vJG698U2Mvo

Stanton, A., Unkrich, L., Walters, G., Lasseter, J., Peterson, B., Reynolds, D., Brooks, A., . . . Buena Vista Home Entertainment (Firm). (2003). *Finding Nemo*.

TEDx Talks. (2013, June 19). *Todd Rose: The myth of average* [Video file]. Retrieved from https://youtu.be/jhXlnvYZZQs

TEDx Talks. (2015, April 2). *Don't believe everything you think: On learning styles and the importance of critical self-reflection* [Video file]. Retrieved from https://youtu.be/855Now8h5Rs

Timperley, H., Wilson, A., Barrar, H., & Fung, I. (2007). *Teacher Professional Learning and Development*. Iterative Best Evidence Synthesis Programme. Retrieved from www.oecd.org/edu/school/48727127.pdf

Vygotsky, L. S. (1978). *Mind in society: The development of higher psychological processes*. Cambridge, MA: Harvard University Press.

Wheatley, M. (2010). *Turning to one another.* Sydney, Australia: Read How You Want.

Wiggins, G., & McTighe, J. (2005). *Understanding by design* (2nd ed.). Alexandra, VA: ASCD.

Index